DRUGS

ANITA GANERI

Edited by Bobbi Whitcombe

Cover illustration by
David Scutt

SCHOLASTIC

"This is an excellent book."

Dr Aidan Macfarlane, Director,

National Adolescent and Student Health Unit.

Scholastic Children's Books,
Commonwealth House, 1–19 New Oxford Street,
London WC1A 1NU, UK
a division of Scholastic Ltd
London ~ New York ~ Toronto ~ Sydney ~ Auckland

First published by Scholastic Ltd, 1996

Copyright © Anita Ganeri, 1996

ISBN 0 590 55281 3

All rights reserved

Typeset by TW Typesetting, Midsomer Norton, Avon
Printed by Cox & Wyman Ltd, Reading, Berks

10 9 8 7 6 5 4 3 2 1

The right of Anita Ganeri to be identified as the author of this work has
been asserted by her in accordance with the Copyright, Designs and Patents
Act, 1988.

ACKNOWLEDGEMENTS

The author and publishers would like to thank the following for their invaluable help, advice and support: Guy Burton and Gordon Eddison of the West Yorkshire Police Force; Paul Watson of Lifeline, Manchester; Nicky Vernon and the Year 10 pupils of Ilkley Grammar School; Christine Weatherill and Gillian Tober of the Leeds Addiction Centre; Dr Puran Ganeri, MBBS, RCP, FRCGP, DCH; and Clare Gibson of Sheffield Social Services. Thanks are also due to Bobbi Whitcombe, for additional research and supplying individual accounts; members of the Suffolk Constabulary, especially PC Terry Broome and DI Geoff Munns; Chris Oakley and Lilias Sheepshanks of Adfam Suffolk; Alan Staff of the West Suffolk Drugs Advisory Service; Dr D.R. Kinnaird of the Bethel Hospital, Norwich; Steve Harris of the North Shields YMCA; Bex and friends, and all those who were kind enough to share their experiences with us.

We are also grateful to all the organisations who sent information (and who are listed in the back of this book).

Contents

Chapter 1

DRUGS

USE AND MISUSE

ABOUT THIS BOOK

You might be reading this book if you have taken drugs or you know someone who has a problem with drugs. You might never have had anything to do with drugs. The aim of this book is to help you make your own mind up. There is information on the various types of drugs, what they look like, how they are taken, what is known about their long and short-term effects, their side effects and dangers. There are also sections on drugs and the law, smoking and drinking and, most importantly, how to get help if drugs do become a problem in your life. People use drugs for many different reasons, and if you decide to try drugs then, book or no book, that's what you'll probably do. But the decision is yours and, armed with more information about what drugs are about and what you might be letting yourself in for, this book might just help you to make up your mind.

'There are two things above all to bear in mind – many drugs are illegal; many drugs can kill you.'
(A former drug addict)

WHAT ARE DRUGS?

'A simple medicinal substance, organic or inorganic, used alone or as an ingredient.'

Well, that's how the dictionary defines a drug but, needless to say, there's a lot more to it than that. A drug is usually

11

said to be a chemical substance which acts on your body and can alter your mood, the way you behave, the way you see and hear things, and how and what you feel. The substance may be simple, but the effects certainly aren't!

But what are drugs, really? What springs to mind when you think of drugs? Heroin, cocaine, cannabis, ecstasy? Drugs come in all kinds of shapes, forms and colours. They include a great range of things, some of which may come as a surprise. For example, you only have to open the bathroom medicine cabinet to come face to face with a whole variety of drugs – aspirin and paracetamol, cough mixtures and cold cures. Even a cup of coffee or tea contains a drug, caffeine, which stimulates your nervous system, making you feel wider awake and more alert. Alcohol and tobacco are drugs, too. In fact, they're such important and harmful drugs that there is a whole section dedicated to them in Chapter Four.

So you are probably already quite at home with a number of drugs. You've probably taken them on many occasions without giving it a second thought. One of the differences between these drugs and things like heroin or cocaine, however, is that aspirin and caffeine are legal. You don't break the law when you take them. And used correctly, and in moderation, they won't do you any harm. In fact, in many cases, the effect of taking such drugs is quite the opposite: medicines not only relieve pain and suffering, they save lives. The exceptions to the rule are tobacco and alcohol – legal, but highly dangerous, drugs both – but more of that later.

The substances you might think of as 'real' drugs, such as heroin, cocaine and ecstasy, are altogether different. It is against the law to possess or take these drugs (see pages 96-109) and their effects can be devastating, even fatal. You run the risk of becoming so dependent on these substances that you cannot function normally without them, and your life becomes a vicious circle of getting supplies of the drug, taking it, feeling good (or bad) for a while, running out, getting more supplies of the drug, and so on. Meanwhile, you have to pay in other ways – drugs don't come cheap, and crime is often the only way of raising the funds. The other danger is that you can never be sure of how a particular drug will affect you at a particular time. For some people, once is enough. They don't live to tell the tale. A depressing thought, but unfortunately it's true.

> **'After a while (not very long), you need the drugs just to feel normal. Then you need more and more of the drugs to keep feeling normal.'**
> *(A drug user)*

SOME BASIC WORDS AND PHRASES

There is a lot of jargon involved in talking about drugs, and a lot of buzz words which aren't very helpful and can be confusing (and, let's face it, the subject is confusing enough to start with). There's a glossary of slang and words and phrases used to describe drugs at the back of this book. But here are a few basic expressions it might be useful to know now.

Drug abuse/drug misuse: when any drug, such as heroin, is used for a purpose for which it is not intended, or when it has not been prescribed for medical reasons.

Tolerance: when your body gets used to a drug so that you have to keep taking more and more of it to get the same effect.

13

Dependence: when you have become so used to a drug, mentally and physically, that you need to keep taking it in order to function normally and cannot stop without suffering unpleasant withdrawal symptoms.

Addiction: when you cannot stop taking a drug, even though you want to.

Withdrawal effects: the way your body reacts when its supply of a drug is stopped. Physical effects can range from headaches to sweating, cramp, uncontrollable trembling and even death. Psychologically, you carry on craving the drug: this can be harder to bear than the physical effects on your body.

Hard drugs: often used to describe very powerful, dangerous drugs such as opiate drugs and cocaine. These are the drugs which are very addictive and physically harmful, and which cause severe withdrawal symptoms when given up.

Soft drugs: often taken for 'recreational' purposes, these are drugs which do not cause strong withdrawal symptoms when not used, but may have long-term effects and are psychologically addictive: soft but not safe.

'Within our society, there are so many double standards at work. It's OK to drink alcohol every day and to excess, but people hooked on heroin are seen as the lowest of the low.'
(A teacher)

Stimulants (or uppers): drugs such as amphetamines, cocaine (and caffeine again) which pep up your nervous system and make you feel very excited.

Depressants (or downers): drugs such as barbiturates, alcohol and tranquillisers which have the opposite effect on your nervous system and can make you feel very low and even suicidal, or very excited, drunk and out of control.

Street drugs: drugs which are bought or sold on the street, illegally. Apart from all the other dangers, you never know what you're buying with street drugs – how strong they are, or how pure or impure they are (see pages 75-80).

Hallucinogenic drugs: drugs such as LSD which cause hallucinations. These are called trips and may result in good or bad experiences, but can be extremely dangerous. Under the influence, you may become frightened or find yourself doing stupid or dangerous things. It is also possible to have 'flashbacks' a long time after you have taken these drugs – a very scary experience.

Designer drugs: drugs which have been specially created in chemists' laboratories, such as the various forms of ecstasy. They are usually badly made and untested, which can make them highly dangerous. One recent batch rotted a part of the brain and caused irreversible Parkinson's disease.

'The consequences of taking drugs are hard to define and doubly dangerous because there are no definites with illegal drugs.'
(A drugs counsellor)

DRUGS IN OTHER CULTURES

Each country and culture has its own drugs and its own traditions and ways of dealing with drugs. Cocaine, for example, comes from the leaves of the coca plant which grows in the Andes mountains of South America. The local Indians have known about the plant as a drug for centuries and regularly chew its leaves on religious occasions and to stave off hunger and tiredness. It is perfectly acceptable in their society – there's no shame or stigma involved, nor widespread abuse. Then, about a hundred years ago, chemists discovered a technique for extracting cocaine from the coca plant leaves, and the cocaine habit was born. The drug became very fashionable in the West, especially among writers and other figures from the artistic world. In bars, cocaine could be added, on request, to drinks such as beer and whisky, to give them more bite! And it was only in 1903 that the coca content was removed from Coca-Cola! Today, cocaine is fashionable with pop stars and sports players alike.

Opium is another drug with a legal and respectable past. It comes from the opium poppy which grows in Asia and the Far East. Even the Greeks and Romans knew all about the narcotic powers of opium, and the opium-based medicine, laudanum, was freely available until the beginning of this century. In the 19th century, opium dens sprang up all over Europe. Here, gentlemen of leisure could recline on couches and legally smoke opium to relax. The lucrative opium trade between China and Britain was actively encouraged. The more sinister spin-off of this trade – heroin – was yet to come (see pages 45-50).

Cannabis is the most widely used illegal drug in Britain. In some countries, however, it is offered in the form of a drink just as people in the West might offer guests an alcoholic drink when they visit. In the Rastafarian religion, cannabis, or ganja, is revered as a mystical herb and is widely smoked for its healing properties. It also provides the inspiration for many reggae song lyrics. This attitude clashes, however, with the law of Jamaica, where most Rastafarians live. There, as here, it is illegal to own or use cannabis.

'Ganja is the East Indian name for herb and, among Rastas, its highest form is called kali, after the Indian goddess in whose honour ganja is smoked along the River Ganges.'
(A Rastafarian)

THE DRUG TRADE

Most people who try drugs for the first time get them from friends, or from friends of friends. They, in turn, buy them from dealers on the street, or in pubs and clubs. This marks the end of a long, complicated chain which, in the case of cocaine, began on the slopes of the Andes far away in South America. The illegal trade in drugs is an international and multi-million pound business. The risks of smuggling drugs overland or by sea to the USA or Europe are enormous, but so are the profits made by the middlemen – the so-called drug barons.

But the drug barons are not the ones who suffer – they just do the organising and let others do the dirty work of growing the drugs, carrying them through customs ... and take the risk of getting caught! Much of the heroin coming into the UK comes via Central Africa where gang leaders blackmail and threaten local people, many of whom cannot even speak English, to swallow condoms full of heroin and travel to Britain with the promise of jobs which usually never happen. Many are arrested and deported; some have a condom burst in their gut and die on the flight.

The international drug trade is a mixture of amateur

risk-taking and major organisational enterprise. The larger organisations use armed gangs, sophisticated communications and surveillance systems, and blackmail or extortion to ensure that their goods get through to the markets. Once in the UK, distribution is by smaller user networks which are difficult to identify and which are generally unaffected by the prosecution of some of their people. Because local distribution is usually by existing drug users, there are always new people waiting to get higher up the chain to where there is better access to drugs. The drug barons have no interest whatsoever in the people their drugs are harming.

Governments and customs all over the world work together to try and beat the drug barons at their own game. Equipment ranging from sniffer dogs to submarines and space satellites is being used in an attempt to stop the trade in drugs. But it's not easy. In Colombia, prying members of parliament and judges have simply been assassinated by the drug barons. Paramilitary troops attempting to destroy cocaine-processing laboratories in the jungle are shot at and killed. It has been estimated that 29,000 people are murdered in Colombia each year, because of their involvement in the drug trade. In Europe and the USA, the Mafia and other organised crime bodies are heavily involved.

> **'2lb of heroin (the same as a bag of sugar) from India or Pakistan will sell for some £750,000 on the streets. It only costs the middleman the airfare.'**
> *(A customs officer)*

The penalties for drug smuggling are severe (see pages 96-109 for more about drugs and the law), more so in some countries than in others. In Thailand, anyone caught trying to smuggle drugs out of the country, wittingly or not, may receive the death penalty if they plead not guilty, or life imprisonment if they plead guilty to the crime. The risks are great, but so are the profits – which is why it is a dangerous world to become involved in. The drug gangs are in it for the money – and to them, other people's lives are cheap.

DRUGS TODAY

The culture of the 1960s, the age of 'flower power', is often connected with the influence of drugs. Peace, love and harmony were in the air, along with the smoke from countless cannabis joints. The aim was to be as laid-back as possible. Some people, famous and otherwise, went too far in their use of drugs. Among them were high-profile stars such as Jimi Hendrix, Janis Joplin, Jim Morrison and Marilyn Monroe, all of whom died from abusing drink, drugs or a mixture of both. Drugs and rock 'n' roll went hand in hand. Heroin became the latest thing in the 1970s and the number of (notified) heroin addicts in England rose from just 54 in 1955 to 25,000 in 1993. Today, the problem of drug use and abuse continues unabated. It is a particularly huge and deadly concern in the USA and, more recently, in Europe. And it's not just a certain group of society or area of the country which drugs affect. Anyone can use drugs, so anyone can abuse them. And the number of people who die from drug-related causes in England and Wales alone is about 25 in any one week.

'One of the guys I see regularly is a marketing consultant earning over £60,000 a year. He needs that much money to fund his heroin habit which costs him £200 a day!'
(A drugs counsellor)

19

'An estimated quarter of 15 to 16-year-olds are involved with drugs.'
(A police survey)

Chapter 2

DRUGS

THE FACTS

QUIZ: WHAT DO YOU KNOW ABOUT DRUGS?

You might think you know all there is to know about drugs. Big mistake! It's often the things people think they know but don't which are the most dangerous. Before we get down to the nitty gritty of the drugs themselves and the reasons why people take them, here's a quick twenty questions to test your drugs knowledge. You could try the quiz once now, then again when you've read this chapter, and compare your *before* and *after* scores. You might be surprised. (The answers – True or False – pages 81-84.)

1.	You cannot become addicted to LSD.	Ⓣ Ⓕ
2.	Injecting drugs is one of the most dangerous ways of taking them.	Ⓣ Ⓕ
3.	Amphetamines are usually injected into the body.	Ⓣ Ⓕ
4.	You can easily take a cannabis overdose.	Ⓣ Ⓕ
5.	Mixing other drugs with alcohol is an acceptable risk.	Ⓣ Ⓕ
6.	People can die immediately from sniffing solvents.	Ⓣ Ⓕ
7.	Crack is a type of amphetamine.	Ⓣ Ⓕ
8.	The first time you try heroin, you become addicted.	Ⓣ Ⓕ

9. It is against the law to pick and eat magic mushrooms. ⓉⒻ

10. Tobacco is more addictive than heroin. ⓉⒻ

11. Ecstasy is pretty harmless to use. ⓉⒻ

12. Amphetamines make you sleep. ⓉⒻ

13. You buy Ecstasy in tablet form. ⓉⒻ

14. Heroin makes you more sociable. ⓉⒻ

15. Kids as young as seven have been known to sniff glue. ⓉⒻ

16. The biggest danger of magic mushrooms is picking the wrong ones. ⓉⒻ

17. Athletes are allowed to take anabolic steroids to make them fitter and stronger. ⓉⒻ

18. People who use cannabis are more likely to go on to use other drugs. ⓉⒻ

19. When you take solvents, you feel drunk. ⓉⒻ

20. People always feel happy and relaxed when they take cannabis. ⓉⒻ

FACTS FIRST

Amphetamines

'I take amphetamines to get me up in the mornings, to make me feel better. Then I take them to keep me going.'
(Chris, 22)

The history

Amphetamines are man-made stimulants which were once prescribed as slimming aids and to treat depression. These days, doctors only prescribe them on rare occasions to treat extreme medical conditions. In World War II and the Vietnam War, troops were given amphetamines to improve their performance! Today, non-medical amphetamines are manufactured in illegal laboratories.

In appearance

The most common amphetamine around is amphetamine sulphate. This is a dull white powder, which you buy in small folds of paper, called 'wraps' or in plastic 'bags'. The problem is that what you buy as amphetamine sulphate is probably only about 3-5 per cent amphetamine sulphate mixed with other substances such as paracetamol, caffeine or soda bicarbonate.

Taking amphetamines

One way of taking amphetamine sulphate is to mix the powder with water or a soft drink and swallow it. Or it can be sniffed or 'snorted' up the nose, or mixed with water and injected. Some people smoke it in a specially treated form known as 'ice'.

The effects

> 'Sometimes you just feel like everything is on top of you and taking some whizz or whatever just lets you rise above it all for a few hours. A bit like going on a mini holiday.'
> *(Vicky, 15)*

The main reason for taking amphetamines is to feel wide awake and raring to go. The drug will keep sleep (and hunger) at bay for hours. It speeds up your nervous system, your heart-rate and breathing. Users become extra alert, extra energetic, extra excited.

Dangers, side-effects, overload

But ... nothing is for free. When the effect of the drug wears off (after about 3-4 hours), you may feel really tired, hungry and depressed. After the initial buzz, it can take a couple of days to recover from the come-down. Your mood swings from confident and cheerful to anxious and irritable. You may also feel extra paranoid and think everyone is after you. Amphetamines can soon prove hard to do without – the two days' come-down may feel like two days too long.

In the longer term, users run the risk of damaging their blood vessels. They may also suffer from heart problems and lack of resistance to illness. And the paranoia can become a serious mental problem.

Aka (also known as)

Speed **uppers** sulphate *pep pills* *fast*
Billy whizz eye-openers **bombers** **truck drivers**

I tried speed after I got bored with cannabis. It made you feel as if you could keep walking and walking and walking and not stop. If you were smoking cigarettes, you couldn't feel the smoke going down. It makes you chew a lot: I chewed gum. You feel really energetic, and you can dance a lot. You'd probably take it at a rave, or something like that. But you can walk about, it's not like cannabis. Everything you see is the same as normal, but you feel different.

You just go up to someone you know does it, and say, 'Can you sort me out some speed?' You get the powder in either a quarter, half or an ounce — it's £6.50 an ounce. You mix it with water, and it tastes disgusting. The effect lasts about a day. It's hard to get to sleep: you want to keep moving, doing something, you're busy thinking all the time.

If you do too much speed, you can have things go wrong: like your liver; you can't do it one day after another. You mustn't do it with alcohol — it could kill you. You'd really freak out, really.
(Barney, 16)

There was this chap we stopped for dangerous driving, and he said, "But I was only protecting my spaceship." He was on amphetamines, *and* his alcohol level was extremely high. He really was not on this planet.
(A police officer)

Cannabis

'The first time I smoked cannabis I got nothing off it for ages and ages. Then suddenly – bang! Colours seemed brighter, the music sounded better. I was just fascinated by everything.'
(A user)

'Cannabis is slightly different from other drugs, but it's often the start of the slippery slope.'
(A police officer)

The history

Cannabis comes from the bushy plant, *cannabis sativa*, a relative of nettles and beer-making hops. It originally grew in Asia but is now found in many other places too. Quite a lot of people grow their own (illegally!). The plant has distinctive compound leaves with serrated edges. Cannabis was used in China as a herbal remedy as long ago as 2,700 BC. It has also been widely used for religious purposes in Asia and the West Indies. A century ago in Europe, cannabis was being used to treat headaches, insomnia and period pains. Today, doctors in the USA and elsewhere are testing its usefulness in treating glaucoma (an eye disease), multiple sclerosis and asthma.

'Cannabis is the most widely used illegal drug in Britain, with millions of users and ex-users.'

In appearance

Cannabis comes in different shapes and forms. First, there's the resin, hash: hard, brown or black lumps of the stuff. Then there are the dried leaves, seeds and stalks of the plant: grass. You can also get cannabis oil: sticky, treacle-like liquid and the strongest form.

The main types of cannabis vary in strength, depending on where they come from and how much of the chemical THC (Delta 9 Tetrahydrocannabinol) they contain. Among the strongest is cannabis from Colombia and Pakistan.

'Skunk weed' is the name given to a genetically altered form of cannabis which is grown under special conditions, often in hydroponic greenhouses (greenhouses where plants are grown without soil but in water with added nutrient chemicals) in the Netherlands and in the south-east of England. It is commonly sold in herbal form or occasionally as resin, and can be between five and ten times the strength of standard cannabis. It can cause temporary paralysis or mild hallucinations.

Taking cannabis

'I don't like the taste of cigarettes so I don't smoke but I really like hash. It gives you a nice feeling. My friends told me it doesn't do you any long-term harm.'
(Gill, 18)

Cannabis (resin, grass or oil) is normally mixed with ordinary tobacco and rolled into joints or spliffs (large cigarettes). This is called 'skinning up'. Cannabis smoke is very hot so a cardboard roach (filter) is inserted in the end of the joint to stop it burning your throat. Other common ways of taking cannabis include 'hot knifing' (sandwiching resin between two metal surfaces and heating them to release the vapour) and devices such as 'buckets' (a plastic drinks bottle which has the bottom removed and is immersed in a container of water for burning cannabis in: this creates a vacuum, and pushing the bottle down forces the smoke out of the neck where it is inhaled in a sudden rush). It can also be smoked in pipes. This way you get a quick effect but you can also regulate how much dope you're taking, and know when to stop.

In countries where cannabis is a traditional drug, people have generally used a water pipe (hubble-bubble or 'bong'), which cools the smoke, thus reducing its cancer-causing heat. Cannabis can be baked into 'space cakes' and eaten or brewed up in tea. This is a bit less controllable – you might end up eating far more than you'd bargained for and feel terrible.

When cannabis burns, it gives off a sickly sweet-smelling smoke – once you've smelt it you can't mistake it for anything else.

The effects

As with everything else, the effects of taking drugs depend on how much you take and how you're feeling at the time. A small amount of cannabis can make you feel relaxed and contented – or just sleepy. Or you may feel uncontrollably giggly, or hungry (the 'munchies'). You see colours and hear sounds (such as music) much more vividly. Or you feel 'stoned' (like being drunk). There's the chance of feeling slightly paranoid and of being extremely sick or passing out if you mix it with alcohol.

'It's a bit like being on a roller coaster – very up and down. First, the ups. Then the great waves of paranoia. One of my mates was in the kitchen buttering toast. I thought he was going to kill me with the knife.'
(A user)

Dangers, side-effects, overload

Cannabis has been known to cause accidents on occasion. As with any drug, users may be less aware of, or careful about, physical dangers. However, the main dangers of taking cannabis are those linked with smoking tobacco – the risk of bronchitis, lung cancer and other serious breathing problems. There have been various studies which show that cannabis smoke is between five and ten times the cancer risk of cigarette smoke. Long-term, heavy users may feel sluggish and unmotivated, and have difficulty remembering things for very long. There are additional risks for people who already have breathing or heart problems; and anyone on the contraceptive pill has a higher risk of heart attack. You're not likely to become physically addicted to cannabis, but you might find it (and the tobacco) hard to give up.

Aka (also known as)

Marijuana hash **dope** *shit*
pot grass **ganja** weed
blow *draw* bush puff wacky backy

(to name just a few!)

When I first did cannabis it wasn't new to me, I was used to it being around my house: my older brother had been around smoking it for several years, though at first I hadn't realised what it was. I started at 15 – I didn't smoke it, I ate it.

That first experience was very strange. I'd no idea what to expect. You have this overwhelming sense of gravity being about 80 times more forceful than it is. Wherever you stop, you get stuck. Your mind stops. You sort of daydream, or drift. It's easy to speak your thoughts. It's just a relaxed feeling, that's it.

If you're with a group of good friends, you might all start laughing and giggling. If you're comfortable with the situation you're in, you open up and can be happy. If you're not, you clam up. Some people chat a lot. For most people, it's like alcohol: it helps them relax. With me, it's the opposite. If I go too far, I go very quiet, I don't say anything. I like to be in control of what I'm saying, and it's better to be quiet if I can't be sure I'll be in control.

Initially it means a lot to you: you become more relaxed, even lethargic. It has an effect on your life at school and, I suppose, at home. Your life at home goes downhill, you become more moody... But I got over that. It actually helped my thinking: I tend to be too logical, and it got me away from a permanently logical frame of mind.

One thing about cannabis is that they smoke it at school – round the back of the buildings and so on. Because it's like smoking, you think you know how not to get caught. But if you get stoned at school, you're trivialising your education. I really wouldn't encourage people to start that early – it does depend on your age. You could ruin your education – and then your life. I didn't get the 'A' level results I wanted because of it ... well, not because of the cannabis bit, but because of the people I was hanging around with.

They say cannabis can lead on to other drugs: well, it's not necessarily the case, but because you get to know more people through it, you get to know the people who deal in other things, so you can get hold of other drugs.

And it's supposed not to be addictive – but it can be. Not many people know this. There was this time when I really couldn't sleep – I went for about two days, and then I had a smoke, and it settled me, and I could sleep. It happened twice, two nights, and then I was all right after that.

I do worry about the generation after us – they're starting younger and younger. I don't think it's good for you if your personality isn't fully developed: you have to be of a certain age to be able to cope.

There's this one kid I know, who's only about 13: he just lives for drugs. It's very worrying – it's a sort of loss of innocence. When it becomes the most important thing in your life – that's not good. It shouldn't be like that. I've seen a lot of people mentally disturbed through it.

With hash, you become more open, it relaxes your mind. But if you're going through some sort of change, your personality's still developing, changing, it's too young. It's really not appropriate to younger kids. You need to have matured, to have reached some sort of idea of who you are.

(James, 19)

I started taking drugs when I was about 12 or 13. I was round at a mate's house, he was 16, and had some cannabis. I tried it and liked it – it's like getting drunk but better. You laugh a lot, and you feel really hungry: we ate lots of chocolate and stuff. It's good when you're watching films, it makes it kind of better: the frightening bits make you jump more, better than if you're sober. You laugh more at the jokes, the funny bits; you get kind of giggly. There's resin, you burn it first, then crumble it up; or weed: you mix that with tobacco, and put it into a pipe. It's smaller than a normal pipe, it gives you a quicker hit that way. Sometimes you can eat it in cakes, or mixed with chocolate. It doesn't have much taste, and a milder effect – it doesn't make you laugh as much.

You have to keep it secret, keep it in a pocket, or I kept it in a private box I've got. You've got to keep out of the way if you're smoking cannabis, or you'll be caught, whereas for drink you can just go down the pub. We'd save it for the weekend. If you do it after school, you wake up next morning with sticky eyes and you can't concentrate as well. You don't think straight.

But beer is £2 a pint, and it takes five or six pints to get drunk: with cannabis you spend less. And you wouldn't die from cannabis (unless you smoked too much, and got cancer from it), whereas with drink, you can die if you drink too much. I don't want them to make it legal, no – it'd probably cost more, there'd be a tax on it and packaging and that. The way it is, cannabis is cheaper.

There are quite a few people I know you can get it from. You get a teenth (sixteenth of an ounce) for £7.50, or a bigger bit, an eighth for £15 – that lasts you 4–5 days. When you're friends with people who don't want to do it as well, we don't bother either: it's not fair on them. But I should think that 70% of the 11th Year have tried it.

After quite a while, about 6–7 months, it got boring. It's not as exciting as it was, really. You can have a laugh – but it's not worth the risk. When my girlfriend found out what I did, she said, 'I don't like you doing it. It might kill you – you might end up doing something stupid,' so I gave it up. Well, I do occasionally still have some, at parties and so on.

(William, 16)

34

Cocaine

'Cocaine is the most lucrative illegal trade in the world.'
(A customs officer)

The history

Cocaine is made from the leaves of the coca plant, which grows wild in the mountains of South America (see pages 16-17). In 1855, a technique was discovered for extracting cocaine from the leaves. Cocaine soon became a popular tonic and pick-me-up in Europe. It was even made into a drink, by the name of 'Angelo Mariano's tonic wine'. Medically, cocaine was used as a local anaesthetic. In the 1970s, cocaine became very popular as the 'rich man's drug' because it was so expensive.

In appearance

The cocaine you buy on the street is a sparkling white powder, made up of tiny crystals.

Taking cocaine

Cocaine is sometimes, not often, injected and sometimes, not often, smoked or rubbed on the gums. It is more usually sniffed, or 'snorted' up the nose. A small amount of powder is put on a mirror and formed into a 'line' (also called a 'hit') with a razor blade. Then it's snorted through a drinking straw or rolled-up paper (if you're being flashy, a bank note). It is absorbed into the bloodstream through the mucous membranes lining the nose.

The effects

Cocaine is a powerful stimulant to the nervous system, like amphetamines (which are sometimes called 'poor man's cocaine'). It can make the user feel great – strong, alert, on top of the world. But the effect is short-lived (about 30 minutes) and users soon need a top-up dose to keep the feelings of tiredness and depression at bay. And so it goes on...

Dangers, side-effects, overload

It doesn't take long to become psychologically addicted to cocaine – the temptation to keep feeling good can become just too much. But people who use it a lot and often may suffer feelings of intense restlessness (the 'cocaine dance'), sleeplessness, persecution, exhaustion and sickness. These clear up when they stop taking cocaine. Snorting can damage the inside of the nose and produce bad nosebleeds – some cocaine addicts have a permanent sniff. A graver danger is mixing cocaine and heroin – called a 'speedball'. This might result in an addiction to two drugs – or it might, more immediately, be fatal. There have also been a number of deaths from heart or respiratory failure because of high doses of cocaine.

Aka (also known as)

Coke *snow* white lady
stardust ice 'C' flake
charlie happy dust *sleigh-ride*

Cocaine used to be known as the 'champagne drug' because only the well-heeled could afford it. But it is starting to become more common in the urban scene, and there's a lot of money to be made from it – and a lot of crime.

Cocaine is produced by washing the leaves of the coca

plant in petrol, which gives you cocaine hydrochloride, which is acidic. It can therefore be absorbed into the mucous membranes (snorted), but can't be smoked (the acid would wreck your lungs). It's water-soluble, though, so it can be injected.

There is a local chap we've seen in here who was a real genius at school, especially at maths; he went on to do brilliantly at college and became an accountant, joined a financial institution in the city and worked the stock market. You can imagine the scene – they're all sitting at their computers, shouting down the phone – and the dealer at the next terminal seems to respond faster, is more alert, risk-taking, gung-ho; he just seems to think faster, he's doing better than you. So, this is your job, your future – you have to keep up with them. Someone tells you how much help cocaine is, and you're away. You can tell the ones who do it, they slip out to the lavatory every half hour or so for a snort. That's about £120–£130 a day.

The career expectancy of these blokes is, they're likely to retire at 30 – after that they're not much good at it, due to the pressure of the cocaine on their system. They've no energy, just can't get up ... that's it.
(A drugs counsellor)

Crack

'The dealers now have runners with mobile phones. They might employ ten runners and pay them one rock for every ten delivered. So the runners may chip a little off each rock and start up their own business. Each of them has a mobile phone so the first dealer shifts vast amounts, but each person only has a little on him.' (*The Guardian*, February 1993, on the growing use of crack in Nottingham)

The history

Crack is simply cocaine in a form which allows the drug to act faster. It is mixed with water and chemicals such as ammonia or baking powder; then the water is evaporated off. This is known as 'freebasing'. The resulting solid is heated so that it can be smoked. It gets its name because it crackles when it is smoked.

In appearance

Crack is sold in small yellowy-white waxy chunks, called 'rocks'. It also comes in white granules which look like powdered milk. The rocks are wrapped in twists of paper or cling film.

Taking crack

The rocks are jammed into a tube, set alight, and the vapour inhaled; or the rocks may be placed on a metal gauze, over heat, and the vapour inhaled through a pipe, or through the neck of a bottle with the base removed.

The effects

'Some users spend £600 a week on crack; one even claimed to have got through £100,000 worth in three years. And it's money they haven't got.'
(*A police officer*)

The effects of crack can be felt within a matter of seconds – in fact, it takes just ten seconds for the drug to reach the brain. Users get a very strong, very intense rush of pleasure and excitement which lasts about ten minutes. Then the trouble begins. The come-down is equally intense. People may get severely depressed or aggressive, owing to the terrible craving for more crack.

Dangers, side-effects, overload

'I regret the first day I ever saw crack. It's cost me everything – the lot. My self-respect, my friends and people I used to know. It's just disgraced me.'
(A user)

You give in to the craving, you take more crack, the high is higher, but the low is lower. Then what do you do? You take more crack... It's a vicious circle of binge, crash, binge, crash. Crack is highly addictive because the after-effects of the high are so unpleasant. Some crack users even turn to other drugs such as heroin to help them 'come down' more comfortably. Regular users may become violent, irritable, withdrawn, lose any self-control or self-respect and be forced into crime to pay for their drugs.

Aka (also known as)

freebase   *flake*

rock wash

rock   **base**   wash

Crack is cocaine combined with ammonia or baking soda, which are both alkaline, to neutralise the acid of the cocaine. It's heated in a microwave till it solidifies, forms rocks which crack when you burn them. You heat them and inhale the vapour, and it gives you a huge high – and then drops you. It only lasts five to ten minutes – the time it takes to burn the rock – and it's very addictive. It feels like an explosion – everything goes fizzy – your brain seems huge, and all your sensations are incredibly vivid and powerful. Your brain seems to be flying, you can think about everything, everywhere, there's this rush of pleasure – it really hits the pleasure centre. It's like the greatest thrill through your whole body, a total physical and mental effect. But it's like amphetamines, you know they say they're supposed to enhance your sex life? Well, that's not true: your mind is so active, your body won't respond. Crack's the same: sex – forget it!

You feel awful afterwards; there's this deep black depression, you want to scream, pull your hair out, do something violent.

Well, I got like that once. I had this clerical job in an office, hadn't done anything stupid or got into trouble before. I'd done a bit of speed and so on occasionally. Then this guy sold me some crack: well, he said, buy £20 worth of speed and you get a rock for free – like a special offer, or loss leader or something. (It's normally £5 a rock – that's £1 a minute.) He said, it's like a really good amphetamine, give it a try. Well, it was. I liked it, and I used to go back to him for more – he couldn't get very much, but let me have one or two bits when he could. After a few weeks, he came back to me and said he didn't know where to get any more.

I kept using it till what I had was all gone. When you haven't got any you feel desperate to get some more, you don't know what to do with yourself, you want to kick something. I'm not normally a violent sort of *person, but when he said there wasn't any more, I went into this kind of blue rage, I became really violent – I went and got this iron bar, and went looking for him, and when I found him I just let out at him, I couldn't stop – if some friends hadn't dragged me off him, I'd have killed him, I know. As it was, he was hospitalised for a week. I don't know what came over me.*

Once I'd got over it, and didn't take any more stuff, it was OK, I was back to normal. But I wouldn't do it again – it was a pretty frightening experience.
(Mark, 21)

Ecstasy

'People take E to enjoy themselves. If you're unemployed, you need something to do. We're young so we don't have any problems with our health. It's safe enough.'
(16-year-old)

The history

The most popular 'dance drug' around, Ecstasy, was discovered in 1912 and used as an appetite suppressant. It was outlawed in the mid-1980s. A word of warning: however much fun it might give, E is a Class A illegal drug, the same as heroin in the eyes of the law (see pages 96-99).

'The media seem to have portrayed Ecstasy as a "fun drug"; in reality, it can kill.'
(A police officer)

In appearance

You're most likely to come across Ecstasy as brown or white tablets or coloured capsules. There are different sizes and shapes, or 'brands', such as Love Doves, Dennis the Menace, Disco Burgers and so on. There is no way you can be sure what a tablet contains. Tablets are often tampered with and other drugs such as heroin added. The side-effects can be VERY unpleasant.

'But E isn't as dangerous as alcohol or cigarettes.'
(A user)

Taking Ecstasy

You start feeling the effects about 20 minutes after you've taken an E tablet and for several hours afterwards.

The effects

Ecstasy is a stimulant drug which zaps you up like amphetamines and gives a heightened awareness, but doesn't produce the distortions and hallucinations of LSD.

Ecstasy has the effect of breaking down barriers and self-consciousness and giving you a feeling of serenity and warmth towards others. That's why it's so popular at dance parties and raves.

Dangers, side-effects, overload

The problems begin when the rave gets going, people take an E and get dancing. They get hotter and hotter. Now is the time to find the Chill Out area and ... Chill Out! E raises the body temperature, and the dancing and the crowded, hot atmosphere at a rave raise it further. Some ravers lose pints of fluids in a single night. If this is you, you need to drink at least a pint of water every hour or so (don't be put off by

Coke being sold at £2 a can – water will do). Remember, drinking water merely counteracts the effect of dehydration; it does not prevent the other effects on the body of Ecstasy, which include raised blood pressure, sudden sweating and, sometimes, a slowing down of the action of the kidneys. So it is also a good idea to eat some salty snacks and drink fruit juice to maintain the body's mineral balance. DON'T DRINK ALCOHOL – it'll make you even more dehydrated.

One of the other dangers with E is 'stacking': this is where an E is taken but does not appear to be working. The user assumes it is a 'blank' and takes another. This may happen several times before the user begins to experience sensations, but because different drugs interact with each other or work at different speeds, they may all start working at once, giving a massive overdose. Symptoms are raised heartbeat and blood pressure, dizziness, raised temperature and blinding headache.

Heatstroke and dehydration can be fatal. If you see that someone has collapsed, call an ambulance at once. Keep them cool. Keep yourself cool.

The long-term damage is harder to define. But this is simply because E is a relatively new drug and has not yet been fully tested, and not because there aren't any long-term effects. There is some evidence to suggest that E may cause liver and brain damage, heart failure and possibly suicidal depression. Some people also seem to be allergic to the chemicals in Ecstasy (it's not the purity we're talking about here) and there is no way of knowing if you might be one of those people – until, perhaps, it's too late.

Aka (also known as)

E MDMA XTC *M25s* Pink Skuds

'I never did any of the hard drugs, I just used Ecstasy and a bit of cannabis at weekends. I used to go to raves, parties and that, at weekends, and I found Es made me feel really good. It made me feel I was the centre of the universe, you know? At a rave, I was the greatest dancer, everyone'd be looking at me, you know, I'd be a really cool dancer and they noticed me and thought, Wow, he's got it! Everything was really going well. The middle of the week was nothing – I just lived for the weekend.

Over a couple of months, I felt more and more out on my own: I think my mental state was changing. I still felt the centre of everything, but it was different. I had this job, driving... I suppose my work dropped off, went downhill. Well, I couldn't get to work on time, I couldn't be bothered, I suppose ... anyway, I gave it up in the end.

I had this feeling that people were watching me: in the street, around me, even from the TV. I knew people were jealous of me, and I thought they were wanting to get me, they were chasing me. This feeling even spoiled the raves in the end – I couldn't go after a bit, because I was afraid there were people there who'd try to get me.

I stopped using Es – I thought that would help. But it didn't. I still had this feeling that people were watching me, after me, trying to get me – to beat me up or something, I'm not sure. I used to stay indoors most of the time, I was too afraid of what might happen if I went out. In the end, I just couldn't go out at all. I wouldn't eat in case the food had been poisoned.

I suppose I just gave up on life. In the end, I was taken into hospital. If they hadn't taken me in, I'd have died. I was there for six months – psychiatric hospital. After that, I still had a long course of treatment: psychotherapy, that was.

It's taken me two years to get back to what you might call normal – so I could even talk to people, you know?
(Michael, 18)

Ecstasy? I've had one at a rave, a couple more at parties. The effect is stronger than whizz – really, really buzzy. You're jogging along on the dance floor, and really buzzing ... or if you're sitting down, it's as if you're just buzzing! You forget all about drinking – you can get very dehydrated. It tastes tangy, metallic, like whizz. The thing about Es is, because they're relatively new, there are all different kinds: capsules, big, little, yellow, pink – you can't tell what you're getting: it could be caustic soda for all you know. I know this bloke who spiked a girl's drink at a night club, so as to get her to dance. She was violently sick, coughing up blood, and then she ended up in a coma for a couple of months.
(Liam, 19)

Heroin

'Do I know any heroin users? All the users I knew are dead.'
(Rosie, 35)

The history

Heroin belongs to a group of drugs, called opiates, which are used medically as painkillers. They are produced from the opium poppy (there's more about opiates on pages 59-60). Heroin is produced from morphine, but is twice as strong. In fact, heroin first came about as a substitute for morphine because, although morphine was an excellent pain killer, it was also highly addictive. Heroin proved to be an even better pain killer but was even more addictive. So the unfortunate morphine addicts went from the frying pan straight into the fire. Heroin got its name because there were such high hopes for this 'heroic' wonder drug. It is still sometimes used medically to treat people with terminal illnesses, such as cancer.

Doctors are obliged to inform the Home Office of anyone they believe may be misusing opiates, or any addicts whom they treat – these are known as 'notified' addicts and may be prescribed heroin or, more likely, methadone as a substitute (see page 74-75). In 1993, there were over 25,000 addicts registered in England alone, of whom 68% (17,000) were heroin addicts. But there may be five times as many people who take and depend on the drug.

In appearance

Pure heroin is a white powder but pure heroin is not what is available on the streets. In fact, pure heroin would kill you in minutes. It is mixed with other powders such as caffeine, chalk, glucose, flour and talc and ends up a lightish brown colour. It is sold in small paper packets, called 'deals' or 'wraps'.

Taking heroin

Heroin can be sniffed like cocaine, or mixed with tobacco and smoked. It is more likely to be heated on a piece of tinfoil, over a candle or cigarette lighter and the fumes inhaled through a straw or rolled-up piece of tinfoil. This is called 'chasing the dragon': the wispy fumes are thought to look like a Chinese dragon's tail. But the most common, effective and dangerous way of taking heroin is to inject it. The powder is usually mixed with water in a teaspoon and heated, then used to fill a syringe. Heroin can be injected just under the skin or into muscles, but the quickest result is to be had by injecting straight into the veins. This is known as 'mainlining'. People start by injecting into their arms, leaving scars known as 'track marks'. But, if these break down (when veins collapse from over use), they will inject anywhere including into their eyes, penises or breasts. Desperate measures...

'When they've been taking drugs people seem happy and have a good laugh. But if it gets serious, like shooting smack, they're not good to go around with any more.'
(15-year-old)

The effects

Taking heroin gives the user a warm, drowsy feeling together with a rush of intense happiness as the drug takes effect. People feel relaxed, detached and free from all worries and cares. First-time users may be sick, especially if they inject. Because heroin is a depressant, it acts like a sedative. It slows down the nervous system, including reflex actions like coughing. Breathing and heart rate also slow down, and the user may become constipated.

'When you use heroin you don't need anyone else – it makes you feel complete and all powerful. You feel totally independent and alone, but you don't feel lonely. First you get a rush in the back of your neck and in your brain and back. And a very strong feeling of contentment and happiness. A total experience.'
(A heroin user)

Dangers, side-effects, overload

Are you ready for this? There are quite a few. Heroin is highly addictive – both physically and psychologically. You might not get addicted the first time you try it, but then you might try it again, and again, and again. Tolerance builds up quickly. Regular users no longer get the buzz they used to. They have to take more and more heroin each time just to feel 'normal'. If they have to go without heroin for any length of time, they suffer extremely unpleasant withdrawal symptoms – cramps, shivering, chilliness, sneezing, sweating. Even when these stop, the psychological craving continues. Heroin users can be very devious when it comes to satisfying their habit, and may turn to dishonesty and crime in order to do so. There are also risks connected with injecting the drug: damage to the veins, gangrene, hepatitis (a blood disease) and worse still, HIV (the AIDS virus). Heroin users whose lifestyle does not include too much attention to their health and hygiene are particularly at risk in this respect. And the heroin they buy may contain impurities which in themselves could harm or kill you.

Last, but not least, there's the danger of overdosing. This often happens to people starting on heroin or to people who have given up for a while, so their body has lost its tolerance, then take their regular dose. It may also happen because of changes in the purity levels of the drug, which the user may not be aware of. Combination with other depressants, such as alcohol, can also cause an overdose. An overdose brings on unconsciousness, coma, then possibly death. If you think someone has overdosed, get them to hospital as quickly as possible. They can then be given a drug to reverse the effects of the heroin. (See pages 148-150 for more information.)

Aka (also known as)

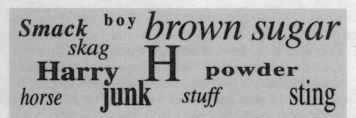

I was 16 at the time I started going out with Darren. He was 19, had left school some time before. My parents didn't approve – well, my dad's got a good job, and they live in a nice house, and I suppose I was trying to get away from all that, so the fact they thought he was a bit rough added a bit of excitement, I think. Well, to be honest, my dad messed about with me, abused me, when I was younger – I'm only just now beginning to be able to talk about this – and maybe I was trying to get back at him, too.

I'd been going out with Darren for a while when I found out he was on heroin. Sometimes he was really rough with me, pushed me around, but other times he was really understanding and kind – said we needed to look after each other. After a while, he said if I really loved him, wanted to stay with him, I should do it too. He showed me what to do – well, he injected for me, actually, I couldn't do it. It was good, in a way: we'd be in a quiet, cosy place, and it was kind of warm and sharing: and I felt that he was looking after me and ... well, I was a bit tense about sex, but this kind of turned me on.

Then I moved in with him, and I looked after the place while he went out to get stuff, and meet people and so on. I knew he was dealing a bit – and he got money by stealing, sometimes. Well, we only got £27 a week benefits and we probably needed about £20 a day.

Then he got busted – and he was in prison for dealing on the street. I didn't know all the people Darren knew, and I couldn't always just go out and get it. I did know some of the people who sell stuff, and I'd be talking to them, and a friend would say, 'Look, you're looking pretty bad, it's not good for you. Why don't you go and get yourself sorted?' And they really meant it – but then they'd say, 'See you next week, anyway' – meaning they'd have some more for me.

After a while, I went to this drop-in centre in the

town, and they came out to the flat to talk to me. They worked with me to help me try to come off it. I got a legal prescription for methadone, which is supposed to help you. It's not the same as heroin: with heroin you get a rush in a few minutes, and the feeling goes on for a few hours, and then you really need some more. Methadone doesn't give you a hit, really; no rush, just a reasonable feeling for the whole day - well, at least it stops you feeling sick. Anyway, it didn't work for me. I went back to the guys I knew on the street and got some more heroin.

In the end, I had to move out of the flat – the rent went up, and I couldn't afford it anyway. I moved away, went to stay with some friends who knew I used heroin, but they didn't. They were really kind. I eventually started seeing another guy, Rick, and he's been really understanding about it all. He's straight, and that helped. I've had quite a bit of help along the way, but I'm OK now. The hardest part was telling Darren it was over. Anyway, he's straightened himself out, too – he went to a drug rehab centre for a while.

(Rachel, 18)

'Two aspirin-sized tablets of LSD would be enough to get well over a million people stoned out of their minds.'
(A drugs counsellor)

The history

LSD (Lysergic Acid Diethylamide) was first produced in 1938

by a Swiss chemist, Albert Hofmann. In 1943, he accidentally swallowed a minute amount of the mixture, and the first acid 'trip' in history began. In his book, Hofmann describes the experience as like being in a 'dream-like state ... with fantastic pictures ... a kaleidoscopic play of colours.' In the 1950s, LSD was used medically to treat alcoholics and drug addicts, and during psychotherapy. It was also used by the US security forces for a sinister brainwashing programme. In the 1960s, LSD became the psychedelic emblem of the hippy movement.

'Why people get hooked is that the first time is so amazingly brilliant. There are lights every-where, figures dancing on the curtains – it's so good that first time, and you're always trying to get back to the first time ... but you never do.'
(Joe, 18)

In appearance

You can buy LSD in tablet form, or as tiny pinhead-sized pills. These are stuck on a strip of sticky tape and cut off as necessary. The most common way of buying LSD, however, is in the form of squares of blotting paper or card, called 'tabs'. These are soaked in colourless, tasteless, odourless liquid LSD. The tabs are decorated with a whole host of designs – smiley faces, Batman figures, cartoon characters etc. One square provides one dose.

'You can buy tabs of LSD at our school for 50p. I mean, they're not really LSD – we just have a laugh making them.'
(14-year-old)

Taking LSD

You 'drop' LSD, in other words, you take it by mouth: it is often just placed under the tongue rather than swallowed. It is such a powerful drug that you only need a tiny amount to get an effect. You might get more or less than you bargained for – some tabs are mixed with other things, others contain no LSD at all.

The effects

LSD is an hallucinogenic drug – in fact, the most powerful hallucinogenic drug there is. Sometimes described as 'mind-expanding', it directly affects the brain so that users see, hear and sense things differently from normal. This spaced-out experience is called a 'trip' and usually lasts for about eight hours. Be warned, though, once a trip has started, for better or for worse, there is nothing you can do to stop it...

'At one point, I was taking acid twice or three times a week. I can say for sure that I knew what it felt like to go mad.'
(A user)

The most important thing to know is that the effect of the LSD depends on how the user feels (i.e. what sort of mood they're in), where they are and who they're with. If you're feeling fed up or a bit twitchy, and don't feel comfortable with the people or the place, there's a real chance of a bad trip with all its unpleasantness – such as depression, panic, dizziness and confusion. A good trip depends almost entirely on a person's state of mind at the time.

Dangers, side-effects, overload

Experimenting with LSD is a risky business. A bad trip

experience can range from unpleasant to nightmarish. You might think you're going mad or are about to die – scary stuff! You might think you're invincible and try to fly out of the window or walk along the motorway. Some people get 'flashbacks' days or weeks after using LSD. They're not usually dangerous but they can be frightening, to say the least. LSD is not physically addictive but you might find the habit hard to live without psychologically.

'Once I had a really bad trip. There was no one there to keep me in touch with reality. The walls and ceiling were coming towards me – I had to get under my bed to escape. I wanted to scream but my parents were in. Then I seemed to be screaming anyway so I gagged myself. It was terrible.'
(A user)

Aka (also known as)

Acid **sugar** blotters
trips white lightning tabs *mellow*

From your first trip, you're never quite the same. Even after I haven't done any for ages, I can lie there staring at something, and it can seem ever so slightly 3-D. The smallest detail preys on your mind. I've become a lot more interested in minute details; I can't stand things in the wrong place. When you do a dot, after half an hour or so, things'll build up and get swirly, and you think this is the peak, then suddenly things explode, everything goes haywire, ceilings running, walls dripping...

The thing about acid is that if you've got something on your mind, a worry or something, it'll magnify itself by a hundred – it becomes a terrible thing, you've got to put it right, or it starts worrying you even more. It's not every time you do it, but if you're in a negative frame of mind, you're more susceptible to a bad trip.

I've had bad trips sometimes. And I've seen people absolutely terrified. Once it was dark, 4 a.m., and the shadows, everything was making a face, sneering, sort of 'We know better than you, we're watching you,' kind of faces. It was just shadows, and then I could see like Egyptian mummy cases – in fact, it was just the trees, but I was terrified... It's just what your imagination does.
(Liam, 19)

'Flashbacks may occur up to three years after the last dose was taken, especially in times of stress. A former client of mine stopped using LSD and got a job in an old people's home. He had not used any drugs for two years when he was woken up by the fire alarm. When he went onto the landing to help get the old people out of danger he thought he saw the whole stairwell ablaze and jumped over the side, injuring himself very seriously.'
(A drugs counsellor)

Magic Mushrooms

'A friend of mine once took some magic mushrooms and he had a really bad trip, he was crying and all sorts, and I had to calm him down. I couldn't relate to this though, as acid and mushrooms are two drugs I'd never try – I don't think I could cope with the hallucinations.'
(15-year-old)

The history
In many ancient tribes and cultures, priests and prophets used hallucinogenic mushrooms to have visions and gain religious insight. There are about a dozen types of these mushrooms growing in Britain. There was an upsurge of interest in using them as drugs in the 1970s.

In appearance
The most commonly used magic mushroom is the Liberty Cap (*Psilocybe Semilanceata*). It grows wild in fields and can be picked from September to November.

Taking magic mushrooms
Magic mushrooms may be picked and eaten raw (legally) or cooked, brewed up in tea or dried for later use (illegally).

The effects
Magic mushrooms contain the chemicals psilocin or psylocybin, both hallucinogenic. Taking them is a bit like taking a mild dose of LSD. Your heart rate and blood pressure increase. A low dose (say, twelve mushrooms) can make you feel happy, excited and detached. A high dose

(about forty mushrooms) causes vivid hallucinations (good or bad, as with LSD). You might also feel sick and have stomach pains.

Dangers, side-effects, overload

The main problem with magic mushrooms is picking the wrong ones – some deadly poisonous mushrooms look very like magic mushrooms. Bad trips are another hazard – you feel frightened and anxious and out of control. No one really knows about long-term effects because mushrooms are not really used long term. You so quickly build up a tolerance to them – the next day you may need twice as many to get the same effect – that people tend to stop using them.

I knew this lad Gary at school, a bit, and then we lost touch. His family were a bit odd. I think a couple of them had to have treatment for mental problems at one time or another. In the end, he left home and was living in a hostel. That's when I met up with him again – and he said, 'Come on out to these woods, I've found a place where you can pick magic mushrooms.' Well, I went with him one time: he had a tent, and built a campfire and camped out there quite often. There was this other older guy, Sid, who'd shown him where to find the mushrooms and what to do, and he was around sometimes.

I went with him once, gathering them – you needed quite a lot – and it was quite exciting, sitting in front of the fire in the woods, kind of at one with nature, I guess. I tried them, yeah. First of all, you get a bit dizzy, kind of detached from the world, with a sort of ringing in your ears. It's as if everything's a bit further away than normal. You see colours – really vivid, and sometimes running into each other, shapes kind of distorted. Everything looks liquid. Noises seem louder –

but it's not easy to tell what they actually are. I didn't do it very much, though, because I was so worried about whether we'd picked the right ones, not poisonous ones.

But Gary went in for it quite seriously, having them as often as he could. He was actually cultivating them in the fridge, in jars, after a while. This went on for about a month, and then he flipped. He went schizoid. He could hear voices, people talking through the walls, and he saw things burning ... he saw the carpet burning, so he couldn't stand on it ... he saw the door burning, so he couldn't go through – he couldn't go out. In the end, he had to go into a psychiatric unit, and he's having to have loads of tranquillizers, doesn't seem to be recovering at all, he was still the same last time I heard.
(Chris, 17)

Nitrites

The history

Nitrites belong to a family of chemicals related to nitrous oxide (laughing gas). There are two types – amyl nitrite and the less powerful butyl nitrite. Together they are known as alkyl nitrites. In medicine, amyl nitrite has been used to treat angina (heart pains) and as an antidote to cyanide poisoning.

In appearance

Nitrites come as a clear, yellow liquid. This smells sickly sweet when it's fresh and like old socks when it's not! The slang name 'poppers' describes the small glass capsules the liquid used to come in. The capsule made a popping sound as you snapped the top off. Nitrites are now usually sold in screw-top jars, often disguised as air fresheners.

Taking nitrites

Nitrites are taken by inhaling the vapours from the liquid. These enter your bloodstream through your lungs and so act very quickly indeed.

The effects

The effect begins almost at once but only lasts for seconds. There is a 'rush' of light-headedness and a feeling of being high. Your heartbeat and blood circulation speed up. People may also lose control for a while and fall over. Then comes the giggliness and carefreeness, and then it's all over.

Dangers, side-effects, overload

Nitrites can be deadly if they are drunk instead of inhaled. They can also cause pounding headaches, hot flushes, vomiting and dizziness. If you spill the liquid on your skin, be ready for it to BURN! Nitrites can cause heart problems in people with low blood pressure and may be linked to certain types of cancer.

Aka (also known as)

rush poppers   snappers
nitrates   *liquid gold*

‘

Amyl Nitrite, when you sniff it, you can feel every pulse in your body pounding, and your skin pumping, thud, thud, thud. You feel as though your head's going to burst; you get this horrible kind of buzz, and a pounding headache for half an hour after you've done it – and it makes you feel sick. It's meant to be an aphrodisiac, but I can't see how. All you get is thirty

58

seconds of sheer hell – as if your eyes are going to split open with the pressure (Es do that as well). You could sniff the whole bottle – and risk a heart attack. If you did something stupid, like get in a fight, run for a bus, or something, you'd probably die.
(Paul, 19)

(Opiates)

The history

Opiates are the group of pain-killing drugs which come from the opium poppy. They include opium itself, which is the dried milky sap of the poppy, and morphine and codeine which are derived from the opium. Heroin is derived from morphine (see page 45). There are also a number of man-made opiates, such as pethidine and methadone, which are used medically as pain killers. Pethidine is sometimes used in childbirth. Methadone is the drug that is used as a substitute drug for recovering heroin addicts.

In appearance

Opiates come in powder, liquid, injectable or tablet form. Raw opium is a putty-like gum. Another opiate, codeine is found in some cough syrups.

Taking opiates

As with heroin, other opiates may be smoked or injected. Opium can be eaten, smoked or drunk.

The effects

Apart from easing pain, opiates bring about a warm, drowsy feeling (see Heroin, page 47). They also make the user very sleepy. In fact, morphine is named after Morpheus, the Greek god of sleep.

Dangers, side-effects, overload

Many of the dangers are the same as for heroin. The opiates are a highly addictive group of drugs and withdrawal symptoms can be very hard to live with. Even under medical guidance, users may become addicted. Other unpleasant, rather than life-threatening, side-effects include feeling sick, constipation and feeling confused. Desperation measures for getting hold of opiates may include stealing from doctors' surgeries and chemists, and may involve the user in an increasingly criminal existence.

The history

PCP (phencyclidine) is a hallucinogenic drug, which is actually made for use to anaesthetise animals in veterinary work. It is much more common in the USA than in Britain.

The effects

Users go into a sort of trance, and feel very small, very light but enormously strong. They may feel numb; their speech sometimes becomes slurred and their vision blurred.

Dangers, side-effects, overload

Too much PCP can cause sickness, convulsions and even, in the longer term, brain damage among users. PCP is often sold as LSD – another instance of not knowing exactly what you're getting into.

Aka (also known as)

Angel dust peace pill

Solvents

'A really horrid way of trying to get high.'
(15-year-old)

The history

A number of substances give off fumes or gas which have
an intoxicating effect. Victorian medical students are
known to have had ether sniffing parties, and nitrous oxide
was a favourite among medical students in the early 20th
century. Nowadays 'sniffable' substances are found used as
solvents in many household and everyday products, the
best known being glue; they may also be gases used in
aerosols, or fuels. 'Glue sniffing' (i.e. solvent abuse) began
in the USA in the 1950s; it became widespread in this
country in the 1970s. Solvent sniffing is most common in
teenagers between 12 and 16, though not all teenagers do,
of course! Some kids as young as seven years old have
been known to try sniffing. Older teenagers tend to move
on to other things, such as alcohol.

In appearance

Things that can be 'sniffed' include glue, paint, nail varnish
remover, correcting fluid (e.g. Tipp-Ex) and thinner, dry-
cleaning fluids; aerosol sprays, e.g. air fresheners, hair
sprays and furniture polish; cigarette lighter fuel (butane
gas), petrol and marker pens.

'There are over 30 sniffable products in an
average home.'
(A drugs survey)

Taking solvents

'I get depressed when I'm not doing it.'
(14-year-old)

There are various ways of 'sniffing glue', though not all of them involve sniffing or have anything to do with glue. Some types of glue may be sniffed directly from the can they come in. Casual sniffers may share a can between four or five of them, and only sniff once or twice a week. Serious sniffers may be on 1-2 pints of glue each per day! Another way of sniffing is from a bag – a crisp bag, carrier bag or something similar. This is held over your nose and mouth and the fumes inhaled. Some people use a bin liner and put it right over their head – very dangerous. This concentrates the effect of the glue. The sniffing continues until all the glue is used up, the glue congeals and goes hard, or the top of the bag sticks together. (There is nothing sophisticated about solvent abuse!) Aerosols are usually sprayed into a bag before sniffing; on occasion, people have sprayed them straight down the throat, but this can freeze your larynx (throat) and is frequently fatal. Fluids can be sniffed from the sleeve or a piece of cloth.

Casual glue sniffers usually get together in small groups to sniff. If you sniff longer term, you're likely to end up going it alone. Your friends will have moved on.

'I didn't feel any pain when I was sniffing; I axed the furniture to bits because I thought I was being chased by monsters.'
(15-year-old)

The effects

The effects of sniffing glue are a bit like being drunk, only it happens more quickly. Solvents depress the nervous system, and part of the effect is because less oxygen is getting to the lungs. You feel giddy, giggly and light-headed.You might also feel sick or later become quite aggressive. You might find it hard to balance, hard to speak clearly and hard to work out where you are. (If your friends start to refer to you as 'that zomboid alien', perhaps you should think carefully about whether it's worth it.) When the glue wears off, you'll probably have a hangover-type feeling for a day or so, and you may find it difficult to concentrate.

'The first few minutes of sniffing always make me feel sick, each time I do it.'
(14-year-old glue sniffer)

Dangers, side-effects, overload

There is a serious risk of suffocation if you put a plastic bag over your head – or if you spray aerosols into your throat: they freeze your airways so you cannot breathe. There can be an effect on your heart and, especially if you do something energetic, you could die of heart failure. Associated risks include loss of feeling: you don't feel the cold or pain so you could easily get hypothermia or injure yourself without realising. You risk accidental death if you sniff in a dangerous place, such as on a roof, near a canal or near a railway track. You might well have no sense of danger, and not notice that you're walking across a busy road. If you become unconscious, you could die from choking on your own vomit.

'I know of one kid who was killed on a railway line – he just sat down on it for a rest. Another was badly injured when he was run over by a car – he was wandering in the middle of a dual carriageway "watching the headlights".'
(A social worker)

'Another kid was saved from falling off the roof by a member of staff who grabbed his leg as he fell. All he could say was, "You can't have my glue; buy your own if you need some. You're not having mine. Let me go..."'
(A social worker)

Regular sniffers suffer from 'sniffers' rash' around their nose and mouth, and also memory loss. However, if they stop sniffing, this can get better. As time goes on, the body develops a tolerance to the solvents, so users need to take more and more. Long-term users risk permanent brain damage, kidney and liver damage.

'You don't think it will kill you; you never think it will happen to you.'
(14-year-old, after attending his friend's funeral)

DRUGS IN SPORT

Another group of people who use drugs illegally are some athletes and body builders. These are the so-called 'performance-enhancing' drugs which not only give their user an unfair advantage over other competitors but can pose a severe risk to the user's health. Many different substances are now banned from use by athletes, including some found in cold cures and hay fever medicines. Athletes need to check carefully what they may and may not use. A list of banned substances is issued to all athletes, though it can become confusing when it comes to treating minor illnesses.

Great efforts are now being made to 'clean up' athletics. Sporting bodies have a system of testing competitors' urine samples for banned drugs, during major games and out of competition. People are tested at random: very little notice is given. Unfortunately, because the pressure to win is so great, some athletes will still take a chance and cheat.

In a survey of top American athletes before the 1988 Seoul Olympics, about half said that they would take performance-enhancing drugs in order to become Olympic champions, despite all the risks to their careers and to their health.

The main types of drugs misused in sport are listed below.

(Anabolic Steroids)

At the 1988 Seoul Olympics the Canadian sprinter, Ben Johnson, won the 100 metres gold medal in a blaze of glory. His celebrations were short-lived. A few days later it was announced that Johnson had tested positive for anabolic steroids and would be stripped of his medal and sent home in disgrace. He received a four-year ban from athletics and, although he took part in the 1992 Barcelona Olympics, was never again the same force.

Anabolic steroids are the most widely abused drugs among athletes and body builders. They are manufactured from the male hormone, testosterone, and are used to build up muscle and strength. 'Anabolic' means 'building up'. Some athletes claim that steroids help them train harder and recover from injury or exertion more quickly. Many feel that, in the competitive and pressured world of sport, the only way to keep up their level of performance and hold their own against their rivals is to take steroids.

Anabolic steroids can be taken by mouth (as pills) or injected. They are sometimes supplied (illegally) in gyms and sports clubs. They are taken in cycles: four weeks on, then several weeks off, for example. But traces of the drugs can be detected in a user's urine for six months after they stop using them.

Dangers and side-effects

Because of the excessive amount of testosterone circulating round the body, there may be development of male features in females, such as body hair, deeper voices and smaller breasts. In males it can cause sex drive and sperm count to be reduced. In young people, steroids may result in stunted growth. Users may also suffer from acne and increased aggression. If the drugs are injected, there is a serious risk of infection. And they may cause liver damage, and even cancer of the liver.

I've been in training since I was about 15. I was very skinny then, 5'8" and eight stone, no confidence, no motivation. My brother took me along to the gym, and then after that I went back with a friend, trained, and really got into it. I used to go after school. I found out about healthier eating, too, what's good nutrition. There were lots of big lads there doing body building, training for shows – if you've got the potential, the genetics, and the will power, you can go far. There are local and national competitions, sponsorship – there's a lot of money to be made.

It all started with a lad going in for a show: he was my training partner, amazing body, good shape – and he asked me to inject him with an anabolic steroid. I didn't want to be involved, but he saw it as just another thing. He said there'd been lots of bad publicity, but so long as you only took the recommended daily requirement it was OK, no long-term side-effects. This was a very educated young man, good job, good background, knew all about the special diet and supplements you need when you're training, drinking lots of water to flush the toxins out, and anabolic steroids are just a part of this.

Then I saw him win the show, though! And there were all these other young lads exploding, bodies blown up! And there was I, I was at a sticking point: I was eating a lot, but not building up fast enough. I said, 'Can you get me some?'

I started on a course of oral steroids, called Stromba. You start on one tablet a day the first week, then two, and on up to four; then you pyramid down. It's because taking all this testosterone makes your own testosterone stop production, and the body counteracts with oestrogen. If you stop suddenly, the oestrogen goes on – that's when you get sore nipples ('bitch tit'), insomnia, headaches, stomach pains, sometimes loss of hair and impotence.

You go on a course for ten weeks, then ten weeks off. In that first course, I went up from nine and a half stone to ten and a half, and lost the half when I came off. So then I went on to a second course, with injections as well: that's an injection every seven days as well as the Stromba tablets. That time I went up from ten to twelve stone, and then lost a half again.

But I was so desperate to get big, to gain more size, I went on to another course. That was a different tablet on top of the first and the injections. You're only supposed to take one tablet a day; and I was getting blinding headaches with this. Someone suggested my body wasn't used to it, maybe I should double the dose. I went on to two and then three tablets, and the headaches went on for about three weeks and then eased off. But my strength was going through the roof. I was eating a lot of healthy food. My muscles developed so fast that my joints and ligaments couldn't handle it. I was getting cracking joints, kind of clicking: if I stretched, my sternum (breast bone), hands and elbows clicked. I had sleepless nights because of the pain. Your legs get stiff and sore: I used two bags of frozen peas to ease the pain and take the swelling in my knees down. The usual pressure on the knees in training on the leg press machine can fluctuate from about 300 pounds up to 1300 pounds, because your strength has been increased so much by the steroids. Tiger balm (a Chinese herbal rub) helped; that has a soothing effect. I'd gone up to fourteen stone by then.

So it went on. After two to three months, I'd lost weight again, so I went back on the steroids; there was Nolvadex, an anti-oestrogen drug; and also Tricarna, a 'cutting' drug, to help burn the body fat off. But four to five weeks after a ten week course I'd get pain when I peed, and I had problems with my kidneys and liver.

The trouble is, in training you're not getting any cardio-vascular exercise (which benefits your heart and circulation system), you're only lifting weights. When you're putting on so much size — I'd put on three and a half stone in twelve weeks — it puts the heart under tremendous pressure. I was in my girlfriend's car, and it broke down on a hill. I got out and pushed it about four metres and I collapsed, with terrible pain in my arm. And then, a friend's dog ran away, and I chased after it: I'd only got fifty metres when I collapsed again, with pains in my arms. I went into hospital and they did an ECG, checked my heart: it was in very poor condition. I also saw a dietician. You see, without any cardio-vascular exercise, my metabolic rate had slowed right down; I was taking about ten hours to digest a meal, but I was eating ten meals a day, and clogging up the system. I wasn't burning up the calories. There was a build-up of cholesterol, which can be damaging to the heart if the arteries fill up with it. The dietitian warned me off anabolic steroids: or at least – knowing that about ninety per cent of people in the sports world are taking steroids – said I should take only the recom-mended daily requirement.

You see, my joints were so stiff that I'd be walking over a bridge or going up stairs, and old people with walking sticks could overtake me! The most embarrassing thing was, when I'd started getting keen on a nice girl, amazing body, we'd been out a few times – and then, I found I couldn't perform. She couldn't understand how I could have done that: she said, 'You're a fool, look what you've done to yourself. This body's not you – a chemist has made that body for you.'

So I really started thinking, If I'm like this now, what'll I be like in twenty years' time? And it was my own decision, I came off the steroids, went on a diet, started some light cardio-vascular exercise, walking, exercise bike and so on. After about six months my heart was in a better condition. I lost weight, but I gradually put it back on again: I'm now thirteen and a half stone, quality muscle, and all natural. They say that you can do the same in three years with natural exercise and training as in one year with anabolic steroids. I didn't do it all in one go: I lacked the confidence, tried another course, and then came off them altogether. I've been natural now for three years. And I've just got married.

Now I've still got a slight defect in the kidneys, a dicky liver (I have to avoid alcohol and caffeine), and a weakness in the heart. My knees are completely shot: if I squat down to do the video, it's an effort to get up – and going upstairs, too. But I can look in the mirror now and think, This is all mine.

I work in a gym now, helping lads in training, and I see a lot of them taking anabolic steroids for the sake of it. It's partly peer group pressure, partly the scene: they see it along with Es and speed, like when they're going to raves – it heightens the natural aggression, and makes them more aggressive dancers. One lad said that when his girlfriend complained he said, 'You wear make-up, I take steroids. It makes me feel better, look better; gives me a good body, more confidence – a tremendous feeling of confidence.'

And it's easy to get hold of. A packet of a hundred Stromba might cost the importer £2; he'd sell it to a friend for £4, and he'd sell it on for, say, £6; by the time they get to the lads in the gym, it would be about £12 to £15 for a hundred. They wouldn't supply them in the gym – it's just that's where people get to know about them. It's all image, trying to impress others: kids will take them. I'd say the most important thing for youngsters is, I wouldn't tell you not to take them – but find out as much as you can about anabolic steroids and their effects. I don't think I was just unlucky: I was fairly typical. At least 45 per cent of people who take them do get side-effects; you need as much information as you can get on how to deal with that. The bad effects will outweigh the good, you can be sure of that. Some people like to take that risk, not knowing – but you have to realise when you take that gamble, you're gambling with your life.

Find out what actually works for you, make your own

mind up; and above all, listen to your own body.
(Adrian, 23)

Stimulants

Stimulants such as amphetamines and even cocaine (both illegal, banned drugs) may be taken to make athletes more alert, more competitive and less tired. In 1976, the lead cyclist in the Tour de France, Tommy Simpson, collapsed and later died. He was found to have been using large quantities of amphetamines to improve his chances of winning – and his body just couldn't stand the strain.

Dangers and side-effects
Stimulants make it difficult for the body to cool down after strenuous exercise. This can lead to dehydration and heart failure. They can also cause loss of appetite and may lead to increased anxiety and paranoia, and the danger of addiction. (See Amphetamines, pages 25–27.)

Narcotic Analgesics

These are very strong pain killers, such as morphine, codeine, methadone and pethidine. They may be used to hide injuries and increase an athlete's pain threshold.

Dangers and side-effects
These analgesics, being opium-derived, may prove to be highly addictive. Because they relieve the pain, they may allow athletes to exert themselves even when injured, so making the original injury worse. Users may also find that they feel sick, have breathing problems, and also suffer from loss of co-ordination and balance.

Beta Blockers

These drugs are used medically to treat heart disease. They slow the heart down and lower the blood pressure. Competitors may use them (illegally) to calm them down and steady their nerves.

Dangers and side-effects

They may cause tiredness and low blood pressure. The heart may even be slowed down too much and stop.

Diuretics

These are drugs which help the body to get rid of fluid. They are prescribed (legally) to people with kidney and heart problems. They are used (illegally) in sport to help competitors to lose weight so they can qualify for a particular weight category and to make them pass urine more quickly to stop banned substances being detected.

Dangers and side-effects

One of the major dangers is dehydration: the body needs a lot of fluid if it is exercising hard. Diuretics can also cause cramp, faintness and nausea (feeling sick); more seriously, they may result in death from heart or kidney failure.

THE DANGERS OF USING DRUGS

Many people who try drugs come to no harm. They can count themselves lucky. Taking illegal drugs is such a risky and unpredictable occupation, you can never be sure how you'll come out of the experience. It could be great: you might wonder what all the fuss was about. Or it could be fatal: you could overdose and die.

If you're going to try drugs, there's a lot to consider, but these are some of the main dangers:

1. Taking too much: You might not mean to, but it's all too easy to take a higher dose than you intend and end up paying the price. You might feel out of control – which can be very frightening – or even collapse and die from an overdose.

2. Becoming addicted: If you carry on using some drugs regularly, and carry on increasing the dosage to keep up the effect, you are at risk of becoming addicted. Drugs can take over your whole life, all your time, all your energy – and all your money.

3. Mixing drugs: It is never a good idea to take different drugs together. There's the risk of double addiction, for a start, and an increased risk of all the dangers and side-effects of taking a single drug. Mixing alcohol with depressants (tranquillisers, opiates, solvents and so on) can, at best, make you sicker than you've ever been and, at worst, kill you.

4. You never know: One of the main dangers of taking drugs is, as we've said before, their unpredictability. It's impossible to say what different drugs will do to different people. It depends greatly on what a particular person is like, what mood they're in, where they are at the time, how much they take, how pure it is, and how the drug is taken (smoked, sniffed, swallowed, injected). If you're feeling really down and uncomfortable with the people you're with, you're asking for trouble. If you feel great anyway, you stand a better chance. BUT since many drugs are mixed with other substances to 'dilute' them, you won't know what else you are taking – it may be different each time – or what effect the combination may have on you.

5. **Physical side-effects:** There are all sorts of side-effects from taking drugs, as you've seen above. You might feel sick, have headaches, stomach aches, and generally be less resistant to illness than you were before. Long-term users tend not to care much about what they look like – the drug's the thing, and everything else revolves round that. There's also the danger of accidents, e.g. road accidents, while you're under the influence.

6. **Drugs and the law:** If you buy, sell or use illegal drugs, you are breaking the law and could be prosecuted (there's more about the Drug Laws on pages 96-109). Not only that: according to some figures, more than 90 per cent of young offenders have been convicted of drug-related crimes. Drug-taking is an expensive habit: a heroin addict, for example, may need £200-£300 a day for drugs. So people may turn to burglary to get ready money.

> **'It's all too easy to be dragged in. Before you know it, you're the junkie.'**
> *(Heroin user)*

Methadone has recently been creeping into the young party scene. That's the medically prescribed substitute for heroin which some recovering addicts use. Whereas heroin is injected, methadone is a green liquid that you can drink. Unavoidably, some gets into the wrong hands, and then it starts spreading into the community. It's a powerful opiate-based drug: it's a depressant, and it's literally fatal to mix it with another depressant. Alcohol is a depressant – but also it's the enemy of the 'Just say NO' approach. After a few pints, you just say yes. When you're drunk you need to be one of the group, be agreeable – and at that stage, if someone passes round a bottle of green liquid... There have been seven deaths from this just in our area in this last year. It's in such an easy form to take. You just fall asleep and don't wake up – or fall asleep and choke on your own vomit.

(A drugs adviser)

IS IT THE REAL THING?

'There's no quality control over the drugs sold; many contain impurities which have a worse effect on the body than the drugs themselves.'
(A police officer)

Just to add to the unpredictable nature of drugs, the drugs sold on the streets are very rarely what they seem. They have often been mixed or 'cut' with other things (called cutting agents) to make a little of the drug go a long way and so increase the dealers' profits. For example, Ecstasy has been found mixed with Vim (cleaning powder) and with rat poison. Many of the cutting agents are poisonous. Other cutting agents include drugs such as paracetamol and caffeine, and substances such as glucose, curry powder, powdered soup mix, gravy powder, flour, baking powder, talc, plaster and brick dust. Drugs have even been found mixed with arsenic, ground glass and human faeces. Lovely!

The names for different drugs vary from place to place, so in a different part of the country, you might not know exactly which drug you are buying.

> *I was at a party with some mates, and one guy had got this really dodgy-looking speed. He seemed quite happy to snort it back, but the rest of us wouldn't go near it – it was yellow! Anyway, for a laugh, we lined up some parmesan cheese in the kitchen. We didn't think he'd fall for it, but he walked right in and snorted it. He was furious afterwards, but we couldn't stop laughing. (I suppose we shouldn't have done it, because he might have choked or something – but there was not very much of it.) He was sick as a dog the next day.*
> *(Martin, 17)*

The other big problem is that you don't know how strong the drugs you're buying are. That's when the game gets very, very dangerous indeed.

There have been a number of deaths recently in Glasgow and Manchester due to excessively pure heroin. You see, as it gets passed down the line from the importers, each person bulks it out with some other substance. These impurities can be anything from milk sugar to cocoa powder – yes, there are different colours: 'China white' is purer, 'Brown scag' is less pure, a mid-brown colour. You end up with a £10 bag, an eighth of a gramme, which could be enough for one or two injections, depending on how strong you want it. Heavy users might use five £20-worth of injections daily.

Anyway, what the end user gets is usually 7%, certainly no more than 10% pure; in the USA it's likely to be 3%. There was this batch that came in, no one knows quite how – you can get gang wars and a load gets stolen, for example – that was 20% pure. Now, most people know their own tolerance, but taking this stuff was like taking double the dose without realising it – which proved fatal.

(A drugs adviser)

'If you get stuff from your mates, you know it's OK, it's safe. And you know that you won't get ripped off.'
(16-year-old)

But your mates don't know exactly what is in the drugs they're selling, any more than you do.

There was this kid who got his college grant, and went and spent £650 on a 9-bar (that's nine ounces) of hash. He went to the coast, and met a bloke in a pub, who said, 'If you give me the cash, I'll be back in an hour'. He was, (amazingly) and the first bloke had his 9-bar – but what he actually had was a big lump of candle wax with hash stuck on the outside! Anyway, in the end he sold it to someone else who was going to cut it with henna, boot polish, road tar, Oxo cubes, that kind of thing.

The thing is, all block (that's resin) is cut. If it's block, you're going to be smoking something else as well. An ounce of heads (of cannabis): you can't cut that. Anyway if you look at it, you can tell, just by the look and the smell. People sometimes use strychnine to cut LSD. It's not just the blokes on the street that you buy from: it's higher up the chain. If a dealer says, 'I've got a reliable source' – you don't know if he's saying that to make money or for real.
(Chris, 18)

WHY DO PEOPLE TAKE DRUGS?

Which of these suggestions do you agree with?

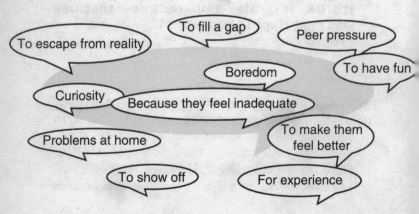

To fill a gap

Peer pressure

To escape from reality

Boredom

To have fun

Curiosity

Because they feel inadequate

Problems at home

To make them feel better

To show off

For experience

78

'Some people just take drugs because the people around them are taking them. If all your friends are doing it, it's really hard not to.'
(Samantha,15)

All the reasons given above come from a group of 15-year-olds who were asked to give their opinions in confidence. Time and again, the words 'peer pressure' were mentioned as the main reason. This means the pressure put on you by your friends and people of your age to do something. It's very powerful and very hard to resist. Everyone wants to fit in with the crowd. You might go along with people just to feel part of the group. Or you might already be part of a group and not want to be left out of whatever your friends are doing.

One way of looking at peer pressure is to see if you can use it in a positive way, to make your friends realise that you care about them and don't want to see them ruining their lives with drugs. It's always worth a try.

'You trust your friends, you've known them for years. But saying no is the easy bit, doing it is much, much harder. You have to ask yourself, is a friendship valuable enough to take drugs for? The answer has to be NO.'
(A drugs counsellor)

'It's usually to do with peer pressure or because they've had a row or split up with someone, or someone close to them has died, or they feel low and have heard that drugs can give them a lift, so they try them.'
(15-year-old)

Most people take drugs to give them a high and make them feel different, although some hope that drugs will be the solution to problems at home or school (which, of course, they aren't). If it didn't feel good, people wouldn't do it. Some people seem able to try something, think about the experience, and 'take it or leave it'; but for others, it may be the start of a serious drug problem.

If you're young and healthy, the long-term dangers and side-effects of taking drugs seem very far into the future – nothing to worry about now. Illness and death are things that happen to old people. Besides, there's the thrill of trying something out ... and of doing something you're not supposed to. Unfortunately, it's not so much fun being caught!

'The risks involved are part of the attraction; people need risks in life.'
(Drugs counsellor)

WHAT THE DRUG USERS SAY

Q. Why do you take drugs?

A. 'I take them to make me feel more sociable, happier, more competent (I don't know if I actually am or not). They make life easier to cope with, for a while.'

A. 'When I'm feeling OK anyway, the drugs don't make that much difference. But I'm hooked on them now so I have to keep taking them whatever I feel like.'

A. 'I tried drugs because I lost my job and I hadn't anything to do with my time. I tried dope first and got into the junkie circle. Then I became a "once-a-week junkie", except that there's no such thing!'

'Many of Dave's friends went to the same university as he did when they left school. So the group stayed together and stayed good mates even when some of them began to experiment with heroin. Dave isn't around to tell his side of the story. He died a year ago from an accidental overdose.'
(Parent of a drug user)

ANSWERS TO QUIZ:

1. TRUE: LSD is not addictive but it is still very dangerous, partly because it is so unpredictable. You can never be sure how it will make you feel and there is the possibility of sudden flashbacks long after you've stopped taking the drug.

2. TRUE: you risk contracting HIV or hepatitis from sharing needles. There is also the danger of skin infections, sores and abscesses, and of gangrene if you inject into an artery instead of into a vein. You could easily overdose if you inject too much. Also, the effect of injecting is more intense and immediate and this, too, increases the risk of fatal reactions to the impurities with which a drug may be mixed.

3. TRUE: amphetamines are most frequently injected or snorted up the nose in powder form; they can also be taken as pills.

4. FALSE: you cannot overdose on cannabis in the same way as you could on heroin. But if you take too much over a short period of time, you could feel very dizzy or sick.

5. FALSE: mixing drugs and alcohol can be extremely dangerous, even fatal. It is never worth the risk.

6. TRUE: some solvents, for example, aerosols, can cause heart attacks (however young and otherwise healthy you are). Solvents sprayed directly into your throat can freeze your windpipe and kill you by suffocation. You also run the risk of suffocating if you sniff glue from a plastic bag.

7. FALSE: crack has a similar effect to amphetamines, but it is actually a form of cocaine which is smoked, whereas cocaine is usually snorted up the nose. Crack is highly addictive with very unpleasant side-effects.

8. FALSE: how quickly you become addicted to any drug depends on how much you use, how often you use it and what sort of person you are. However, heroin is a highly addictive drug. If people have a good first experience with it, the chances are that they will try it again. By the time they have a bad experience, it is too late and they are hooked.

9. FALSE: it is legal to pick and even eat magic mushrooms in their raw state but it is illegal to process them, i.e. to dry them, cook them or make them into tea.

10. TRUE: believe it or not! Tobacco contains nicotine which is one of the most powerfully addictive drugs known (there's lots more about tobacco and smoking on pages 120-129).

11. FALSE: there have already been more than 50 deaths from Ecstasy. Many are due to heatstroke and dehydration caused by using ecstasy at raves; some are due to the direct action of the drug on the individual user's metabolism. So it is far from harmless although, being relatively new on the scene, there has not yet been time for much research into its long-term effects. Scientists do think, however, that it could cause liver damage and brain damage.

12. FALSE: people take amphetamines (speed) to give them a rush of energy and keep them awake. But the energy is only on loan, so the answer is TRUE to an extent. When the effects of the drug wear off, people feel very tired and lethargic, and may need extra sleep for several days to recover.

13. TRUE: Ecstasy is sold and taken in tablet form. The danger is that you never know exactly what each tablet contains – the Ecstasy is often mixed with other substances to make it go further and increase profits. There's no such thing as quality control. You're in big trouble if it's been mixed with something like rat poison, but you've no way of knowing until it's too late.

14. FALSE: heroin users are often very anti-social. They feel that taking heroin is such a complete experience that they do not need outside contacts, and withdraw into their own world. They can become completely detached from any sense of pain, hunger or anxiety.

15. TRUE: unfortunately, very young children have been found sniffing, and dying from solvent abuse. But the peak age for sniffing seems to be 13-14; older teenagers don't seem interested. A depressing statistic is that of the hundred or so solvent-related deaths a year, a quarter of these are first-time users.

16. **TRUE:** the biggest danger is that instead of a magic mushroom you may pick a highly poisonous species, such as a deathcap, instead. As its name suggests, even a small piece of this mushroom can kill you.

17. **FALSE:** athletes are not allowed to use 'performance-enhancing' drugs. If they are caught using them, they can be disqualified and banned for life from the sport. Remember Ben Johnson in the 1988 Seoul Olympics?

18. **TRUE:** they are more likely to try other drugs but not all cannabis users do so. The danger is that becoming involved in one type of drug gets you involved in the world and culture of drugs and drug users and you may find it very difficult to get out or say *No* to other drugs.

19. **TRUE:** you feel drunk but far more quickly than you would if you drank alcohol. This is because the chemicals from the solvent travel into your bloodstream from your lungs, rather than from your stomach (as in the case of a drink). One of the dangers of this is that you become intoxicated before you realise it and could hurt yourself.

20. **FALSE** – not everyone feels happy when they take cannabis. Some people have severe attacks of anxiety, especially if they are already anxious or worried.

Chapter 3

DRUGS

THE CONSEQUENCES

ADDICTION

'They seem fine on the surface but then you realise they've been lying to you about everything. They become so devious and untrustworthy. Destructive, above all. And there's this odd set of rules. They don't steal from friends, only from strangers. At first, that is. After a while, anything goes.' *(Someone who used to live with a heroin addict.)*

Taking drugs is one thing; leaving them alone can be quite another thing altogether. It must be said that the number of people who use illegal drugs regularly in this country, let alone become addicted to them is, fortunately, quite small. But that's no reason to become complacent or think it won't happen to you. Because, if you take drugs, the risk is always there!

'You felt as if you'd golden fire running through your veins. That's not easy to fight against.' *(A drug addict)*

Addiction is said to be when someone comes to depend on a drug or the experience they have whilst on drugs. In other words, they need the drug so badly that they can't do without it. And there are some very unpleasant effects on withdrawing from it. To cope with that takes quite a lot of courage. The dependence can be physical and psychological. Even when the physical symptoms of withdrawing from the drug are over, usually in a few days, you carry on craving the drug and that can be a very powerful incentive to take it again. Addiction is when drug-taking gets out of control, when you can no longer stop it and don't know if you would even if you could. The drug takes over – all your time, energy and money are spent on getting hold of the next supply. The urge to take the drug becomes overwhelming: far, far stronger than ordinary will power. Nothing else matters except satisfying the craving.

Not all drug addicts are scruffy, homeless and unemployed, however much this might be the stereotype. Some hold down good jobs, live their lives and keep their habit pretty well hidden. But the risk that your life might fall apart around you, and the danger of letting yourself go completely, are part and parcel of the whole scene.

So, how do people become addicted to drugs? There's not really an easy answer to that question. Most people who take drugs take them to make them feel good, to give them a buzz or a high. If they like it, there's a good chance they'll try it again. If they are taking drugs to escape from their problems for a while, they might try them again if the problems don't get any better or don't go away. It won't solve the problems, but it might make them seem less depressing for a while. There's also the problem of coming down from the drug: this can be a pretty gloomy experience, only relieved by another fix and another high.

Of course, it's not as straightforward as high, low, high, low. Your body can get used to almost anything and tolerance to a drug can develop quickly (see page 13). The dose you've been taking is no longer enough, and you need to take bigger and bigger amounts to get the same effect. Sooner or later, even this is no longer possible and you take the drug in order to feel normal, not to feel high any more. Or you move on to something stronger.

'To me, being addicted to drugs means being completely trapped by them. I need them to function. I've got no control. I get up in the morning and mark time until I can get hold of a fix.'
(A drug addict)

Drug addiction doesn't happen overnight. But it doesn't take long. It's estimated that if you took a regular dose of heroin for example, every day, you'd be addicted to the drug in about two weeks. If you gave it up then, you'd probably experience mild withdrawal symptoms, similar to the symptoms you get with flu. In general, the longer you take a drug for and the more you take, the worse the withdrawal symptoms. It can take years to recover from addiction, if you ever do.

I met Angela in my first job. We got on well, we could really talk to each other and we had a lot of fun. Some of the people we worked with were really boring. Our jobs were boring, too. She was a filing clerk, I was a typist. We both knew we could do something a bit more interesting.

Angela never seemed to have the energy to try, though. In the end she lost her job. The company didn't want to sack her. They liked her. She was a sweet person – but she wasn't into the work. So they gave her a bit of a handshake to go off and do something else. They sort of hoped she'd get a bit of training to do something better.

She never got another job. Well, not for a long time,

anyway. It got really hard to keep in touch with Angela after she left. Sometimes we'd arrange to meet and she'd be two hours late. Other times she didn't turn up at all. I just thought she couldn't be bothered, and I started to get really annoyed.

One time we did meet, she started to tell me about her habit. She said she'd got interested because it seemed like it might be a good 'way out'. She'd had a lot of family problems that had left her feeling unloved and unwanted, so she wanted the option to end it all if she needed to. That was the story she told me, anyway.

She started out by snorting heroin, and that was OK. It seemed to take away all her problems. It made everything all right. It was one way of carrying on, but it just made getting up every day that bit more difficult. And coming to see me was an effort she couldn't always manage.

But she got in on the scene, and was mixing with all kinds of people. Inevitably, someone eventually persuaded her to inject. Then the rot really set in. She wasn't working. The payoff from the filing job was long gone. She didn't have the energy to find herself a job. So she started shoplifting.

I hadn't heard from her for a while, when I got a call in my new job. 'I've got to go to court tomorrow. Please will you come?' So I did. I didn't really know what to expect. What she was expecting was that I'd pay £500 bail. I didn't have the money, and I couldn't have taken that responsibility, to have to get her to court, anyway. In the end she was kept on remand instead. I have to admit I was pretty relieved.

She was ten months awaiting trial. I visited when I could, and wrote. She tried to persuade me to bring in some heroin on cell visits. I could pass it to her mouth to mouth. I didn't dare.

Eventually, she got a suspended sentence. I thought the one good thing was that she'd got off the drug. She *came to live with me.*

It all went really well to begin with. She was so pleased to be out and so grateful. She didn't do much about finding a job at first, but in the end she got some shop work and seemed to be OK. She made new friends and started applying for serious jobs.

We let her stay on condition that none of her old friends came round. She said that was fine, but we weren't there all the time. Who knows what happened when we went on holiday?

Everything seemed fine on the surface, but it was the little things that started to make me suspicious. I'd come home to find things had moved slightly. A full gin bottle would be half filled with water. Eventually, she moved a friend in with her. Just for a few days to start with, but the friend never seemed to go. They'd stay in Angela's room for hours and creep in and out of the flat, hoping we wouldn't notice them, and wouldn't stop them to ask what was going on. We started to feel uncomfortable in our own home.

Then things started going missing. Nothing major. I had a feeling they knew where everything was. Even the spoons were going missing. I thought we were imagining it at first. Then some spoons started to appear again, and there'd be strange kinks in the handles where they'd been bent back.

I knew something was going on, but I hadn't a clue what to do. I bought books that told me what to look out for, but you can only really prove someone's on heroin by looking closely at their eyeballs, or testing a urine sample. How was I going to do that? It went on for weeks. I tried to talk to Angela about it, but she always had an amazing and plausible explanation for everything. I've never known such an inventive liar. It got so I couldn't believe anything she told me. And I was turning into a nervous wreck.

Eventually, they took something from my room and I

lost my cool completely. I threw Angela and her friend out of the house. We tried to stay friends for a bit, but I was so suspicious. Her friend really had it in for me, and I couldn't handle seeing the two of them together. If Angela hadn't been mixed up with other users, I feel I might have been able to help her. But there was such a network of people, I couldn't begin to compete.

I used to hear that people had seen her around the town, but no one seems to have seen her for a few years now. I don't know if she's dead or alive. And I still feel terrible guilt. I could have helped her if only I'd been strong enough, if only I'd known how. She wasn't a bad person. She was sweet and sensitive and caring. And, once upon a time, she was a really good friend.
(Jane, 24)

'I'M NOT ADDICTED, AND I DON'T NEED TREATMENT'

Every five minutes, in the USA, a baby is born who is already addicted to crack, via the drugs in its mother's bloodstream.

> **'The word was out [on heroin and crack]. I knew if I got mixed up in them, I wouldn't be able to stop.'**
> *(A cannabis user)*

Hardened addicts can make their own and everybody else's lives utterly miserable. One of the biggest obstacles to helping them is that they may completely deny that they have any sort of problem with drugs. They may become hostile or even violent if you suggest they should get help. There's also the problem of funding their habit – people may get into the habit of stealing and lying in order to pay for drugs. This can be very hard for friends and family to handle.

There are 14 notifiable addictive drugs, including heroin, cocaine (and crack), methadone and morphine. The most common addictive drugs are heroin and cocaine, especially crack cocaine. In Britain, there are about 28,000 drug addicts registered with the Home Office. (Doctors who give treatment to addicts have to notify the Home Office. These addicts are then under some kind of medical observation and able to get help and advice.) However, it is estimated that this only represents one in five of all regular users.

'Taking drugs doesn't necessarily mean addiction which doesn't necessarily mean death – but there is always that possibility.'
(A drugs counsellor)

'The bad thing is that you don't have time for anything else – you're tied by your habit. But if you're addicted to drugs you put up with the inconvenience. The drugs are more important than anything else in your life.'
(A drug addict)

DRUGS AND AIDS

The first AIDS sufferer in Britain was diagnosed in 1981.

Ten years later there were, officially, almost 5,500 people with AIDS. Over half of them were already dead.

You already know about some of the consequences of getting mixed up in drugs: the lack of control over your own life, the damaging effect your habit can have on other people's lives, the risk to your health and the possibility of getting involved in crime (there's more about the drug laws later in this chapter). There are all sorts of consequences for a regular drug user. One of the most worrying of recent times is the risk of contracting the HIV virus from contaminated needles.

It's not just heroin addicts who are at risk. The HIV virus can also be spread by sharing needles to inject anabolic steroids.

For many long-term drug users and addicts, the most effective way of taking drugs such as amphetamines and heroin is to inject them into their veins. However horrible this may sound, there is not usually a problem if the needles used are clean and sterilised. The problems start if the needles are dirty or contaminated. It is estimated that two thirds of all drug injectors may carry Hepatitis C, a potentially fatal liver disease which is very easy to pass on through sharing injecting equipment including spoons, filters and water.

AIDS (Acquired Immune Deficiency Syndrome) is caused by a virus (the HIV – Human Immunodeficiency Virus). This virus damages the body's natural defence system, the immune system, which usually protects us automatically from many different types of disease and illness. If it is damaged, we no longer have that strength of resistance. People with the HIV virus may be perfectly healthy for many years before full-blown AIDS and the illnesses associated with it develop. Although a great deal of research is being done into the causes and treatment of AIDS, there is, as yet, no cure.

Once someone is infected with HIV, they are infected for ever and they can pass the virus on to other people. The

HIV virus can be spread from person to person in infected blood, which is why sharing needles is so dangerous. Users are not likely to know if the other people they're sharing with are infected or not. The best way to be safe (apart from not injecting in the first place!) is for each user to keep and use his or her own needle and syringe. Addicts can also take used needles to the network of needle-exchange schemes which have been established all over the country. Here they can dispose of dirty needles safely and exchange old needles for new ones.

AIDS is also commonly spread in body fluids passed on by having unsafe sex. It's easy to forget about wearing a condom if you're stoned or high – but it could save your life or someone else's. So it is really important to think about using a condom before you get to that point.

To find out if you might have been infected with HIV, you can have a test. You may need to have another test three months later because it takes this length of time for the antibodies (which your body makes to fight the virus) to show up. A positive test means there are antibodies present, hence the term 'HIV positive'. Tests are best done at a Genito-Urinary Clinic (clinic for sexually transmitted diseases), or you can get advice from your local drugs service. Never accept the offer of an HIV test unless you are first offered counselling about what it involves and what the results mean.

Although people with HIV may look healthy and well, the virus continues to multiply inside them, attacking and destroying their immune systems. Eventually, their immunity becomes so low that their health is at serious risk from diseases such as pneumonia, cancer and kidney failure. A person who develops one of these illnesses is said to have full-blown AIDS.

The virus can even be passed on from an infected mother to her baby. This can happen while the baby is still in her womb.

So, the message is simple:

DON'T INJECT DRUGS,

If you do inject,

DON'T SHARE NEEDLES,

DON'T HAVE UNPROTECTED SEX.

DRUGS AND THE LAW

Every year about 40,000 people are arrested by the police for drugs offences. Some are big time crooks who make their living from drugs. But the great majority of those arrested get caught with a couple of Es or some cannabis.

If you use drugs at all you may be breaking the law and risking prosecution and a prison sentence for doing so. Britain has strict laws concerning the possession and sale of illegal drugs. Anyone who uses illegal drugs runs the risk of getting caught with them and being arrested for it. Most people are arrested for possession of drugs. This means the drugs are intended for their own use. Far more serious, in the eyes of the law, is possessing drugs with the intention of supplying them to other people. This includes you giving your friend an E tablet, or even intending to give your friend an E tablet. You might not think that you're drug dealing, but you are. And it's a crime which can carry a hefty prison sentence.

'I never thought it could happen to me. First of all, I didn't mean to try drugs. Then I didn't mean to end up a criminal. But I managed to do both.'
(16-year-old)

The main law against drugs is called the Misuse of Drugs Act 1971. This is intended to stop the use of drugs for non-medical purposes. It divides drugs into three different classes – A, B and C. Class A is the most serious and carries the most serious penalties, even life sentences; Class C carries lesser penalties. You can see how the Act works in the table below:

THE MISUSE OF DRUGS ACT

CLASS A DRUGS:
Heroin, Methadone, Opium and other strong opiates
Cocaine, Crack
LSD
Ecstasy
Cannabis oil
Processed (i.e. dried or cooked) magic mushrooms*
Any Class B drugs which are taken by injection

PENALTIES (MAXIMUM):
Possession – 7 years in prison, plus a fine
Possession with intent to supply ('pushing' or dealing) – Life imprisonment, and unlimited fine, which can include sequestration of assets (seizure of your possessions)
Trafficking/importation and manufacturing – Life, plus unlimited fine
Allowing premises to be used for drug-related activities – 14 years plus a fine

'I was sorry, I really and truly was sorry. But it didn't stop me being sent to prison.'
(Convicted E dealer)

* It is not against the law to pick magic mushrooms or to eat them raw. But anyone caught giving another person magic mushrooms is potentially committing an offence for which they would be tried in a Crown Court and could face up to 14 years in prison.

CLASS B DRUGS:
Amphetamines
Barbiturates
Cannabis resin and herbal cannabis
Codeine and weak opiates

PENALTIES (MAXIMUM):
Possession – 5 years in prison, plus a fine
Possession with intent to supply – 14 years, plus a fine
Trafficking/importation and manufacturing – 14 years, plus unlimited fine
Allowing premises to be used for drug-related activities – 14 years, plus a fine

CLASS C DRUGS:
Tranquillisers (e.g. temazepam)*
Mild amphetamines
Some painkillers (such as the codeine-based DF 118)

PENALTIES (MAXIMUM):
Possession – 2 years in prison, plus a fine
Possession with intent to supply – 5 years, plus a fine
Trafficking/importation and manufacturing illegally – 5 years, plus an unlimited fine
Allowing premises to be used for drug-related activities – 5 years, plus a fine

* There is more about tranquillisers on page 113-115. It is illegal to supply them to other people for non-medical use but not illegal to use them yourself without a prescription. (IT'S STILL DANGEROUS, THOUGH!)

'Lots of my friends do drugs. Even the threat of being shopped to the police doesn't have any effect on them.'
(18-year-old)

As we said at the start of this chapter, don't think it couldn't happen to you, because it could. And it might affect the rest of your life. Even being cautioned by the police means a criminal record.

The police have very wide powers when it comes to drugs, even though they do not detect every offence committed. They can stop people in the street and search them for drugs. They can search people's homes. Police forces up and down the country work together to exchange information. They are also in touch with police forces abroad, and with the customs and excise officers who patrol places like airports and ports, where drugs might be smuggled in from abroad. The police are mainly concerned with catching the drugs dealers, many of whom never take drugs themselves but are in it solely for the money.

Police officers sometimes go undercover to infiltrate the world of the dealers. They are helped a good deal in their investigations by informants. Most of these people are involved in the drugs world, in one way or another. They may be out for revenge, or need the money, or simply be in it for the thrill. Their information is very useful; but the consequences of giving it may be fatal, if the dealers involved find out who is responsible. Violence has become a big part of the illegal drugs scene.

My first, and I'd say worst, experience was a few years ago, when I was a uniformed officer in London, working nights in the King's Cross area. We were called out to a disturbance at a party in a block of high-rise flats. When we got there, there was a 15-year-old girl on the ground at the foot of the block, smashed to pieces. The party was on the eleventh floor, and they'd all been having a good time, and this girl had been given an LSD tablet, persuaded by her friends that it would be good for her. She'd been on a trip for about an hour and a half, and it was a bad one: it depends what mood you're in how it affects you. She'd vomited badly, and been clawing at herself - and then she'd told her friends that she could fly.

The worst thing, I think, was that her body had bounced off the walls of the block as she fell; it was 5.00 a.m. and as the light rose, you could see the pigeons pecking at the bits of flesh on the walls.

More recently, there was a 14-year-old boy at a party: he'd been drinking a lot and then someone gave him a 'cocktail' – with amphetamine tabs in. Having it on top of the alcohol made him violently sick; but it produced a rush of all the sensations, as amphetamines would. Now, this was a perfectly fit lad. He died of a heart attack.

I would say that although I work now in a comparatively rural area, the drugs problems around are much the same wherever you are – with the exception of the very deprived inner city areas, where you've got more serious drug-related crime. I think LSD is very much on the increase, along with crack cocaine.

There are three types of people who get involved with drugs:
1. The ones who have a one-off experience – this might be one in three under-25-year-olds.
2. The 'social' users: they use cannabis, amphetamines and Ecstasy (and, occasionally, heroin and cocaine).
3. The addicts – a very small minority.

The way the police work is through Customs and Excise, who aim to stem the import of drugs; the regional Crime Squads, who try to deal with the major distributors; and the local force Drug Squads, who are dealing with the dealers. Street-level dealing is dealt with by local police officers, and so are users. I suppose first-time users or people found in possession would get a caution, and upwards from that.

One of the big problems is the things people will do to make money out of drug use – like diluting them. There have been people we've arrested for dealing in Ecstasy pills, selling them for £10 to £25, and they've turned out to be paracetamol. Worming tablets, bicarbonate of soda – they'll add all kinds of impurities to make more money. Another thing is, at raves, for example, if the kids are taking Ecstasy or amphetamines – it's fatal to mix them with alcohol – they need 'chill-out' sessions, to have a drink and cool down, and unscrupulous dealers will sell bottled water at ridiculously inflated prices.

The thing is, kids know about the buzz, the fun, but there's not enough information available on the down side, the long-term health effects of 'social' drugs. They don't see the harm in 'having a go'. And drugs work quicker than alcohol: the average person can't drink a bottle of whisky every night, but you could take an Ecstasy tab every night – and kill yourself.

And it's just as easily available. A cannabis joint would cost you, say, £1 to £1.50. The effects might last you two to three hours. Smoking five cannabis cigarettes a week would mean you'd taken in the tar content equivalent to smoking 20 cigarettes a day – with all the associated risks of smoking-related diseases. The main ingredient, THC (Tetrahydrocannabinol), leaves a residue in the body which can stay for three to four weeks, and can build up a deposit. With habitual use, you can get short-term memory loss, and physical impairment.

101

Amphetamines: one gramme 'wrap' costs about £10; an Ecstasy tab up to £25; LSD, a tab might be £5 to £10. Now, that can cause flashbacks for up to seven years. Some people now do LSD in organised groups. One person doesn't do the drug, so as to keep an eye on the others.

The vulnerable ones are those kids round the 14 to 16 age range. It's not just drugs: they're vulnerable in all sorts of ways. It's easy to succumb to peer pressure. What seems to be the attraction? It's the thrill. Someone they know, look up to, maybe a bit older, says it's good. There's a group of about twenty kids hang around this town, down at the corner, in the evenings, and the ages are anything from 15 or so up to about 25. They're mainly just talking, hanging around, not doing any harm – but that's one of the ways they get to hear about it, and maybe have a go. They've been to classes where they've been told about it, heard of the dangers, know the theory – but they're interested in the thrill: it's fun! And drugs are easily available – far more so than when the older generation were that age. Most kids are aware of the dangers of mixing drugs with alcohol – they'll be careful about that.

Many drugs (except cannabis, Ecstasy, amphetamine sulphate and LSD) are available on prescription: it's the misuse that we're concerned with. Under the Misuse of Drugs Act 1971, drugs are categorised, and the penalties range from up to two years for possession of Class C drugs, up to life and an unlimited fine (which can include sequestration orders on homes, cars, etc.) for possession with intent to supply for Class A drugs. And allowing premises to be used (like, say, parents letting kids use the house for a party) – it's the same degree of crime as possession with intent to supply. For manufacturing and importing it can be up to life, as well.

My own personal feeling is that the drugs problem won't go away until it's socially unacceptable. The kids'll go on

using them – will society change, or will they? Do you need to use a 'big stick' – or some kind of shock/horror campaign, so everyone is really familiar with the dangers and problems? Like, for example, many kids are very aware of the dangers of drinking and driving. Everyone is aware of the premature deaths and accidents caused by drink and smoking: we need a similar awareness about drugs.
(A police officer)

THE LAW AND SOLVENTS

It is not illegal to buy, possess or to sniff solvents. But solvent users may be arrested and convicted for unruly behaviour, likely to cause a 'breach of the peace'. It is illegal, however, for shopkeepers to sell solvents to anyone under the age of 18 if they think they might be intending to sniff them – not always an easy thing to decide.

THE CASE FOR LEGALISING CANNABIS

'It's a lot less harmful than whisky, or nicotine, or glue.'
(A pop star)

'If it is legalised, it must be licensed and there must be quality control and plenty of information about it.'
(A drugs worker)

There have been many arguments for and against making cannabis a legal drug, just as tobacco and alcohol are legal drugs. At the moment, cannabis is strictly controlled by the law. It is illegal to grow, produce, possess or supply the drug, and to allow it to be grown or used on your premises.

The case for: Some people argue that cannabis is far less dangerous than tobacco. It isn't addictive (whereas tobacco is) and legalising it would allow the police and other authorities to concentrate on stopping the trade in more dangerous drugs, such as cocaine and crack. At present, about 80 per cent of all drugs offences in Britain are related to cannabis. An individual is entitled to make his or her own choices as they do about tobacco, they argue, without the state controlling what they do in private. If we give people enough information, they say, they'll avoid using dangerous drugs.

The case against: On the other hand, others argue, a drug is a drug is a drug. If we give serious consideration to legalising one drug, will we need to consider legalising others, too? And they worry about the potential of cannabis to introduce people to the whole drugs scene and to the world of more dangerous and sinister drugs. There is also the problem of not being able to control who obtains it, so young children might have access to the drug; and the probability that those people who are in business marketing cannabis for profit would want to get as many people as possible to use it. Alcohol is a legal drug, people argue; there is plenty of information about the dangers attached to it – but has that stopped people using it? Alcohol is the most widely abused drug in the UK. Perhaps the State has a responsibility to protect individuals from substances which can seriously damage their health. The argument is a highly complex one.

'How would you feel about flying if you knew that the pilot had been using cannabis before taking off?'
(A drugs counsellor)

The police are now tending to punish cannabis offences with fines rather than with prison sentences, but the fact that the drug is illegal still means that, if convicted, you get a criminal record which could affect your education and, later on, your career. In Holland, the police have been much more liberal in their attitude towards cannabis users. They do not believe that sentencing someone to prison does anything to control the use of the drug. The possession of cannabis stopped being a criminal offence there in 1976. There are even some cafés in Amsterdam where cannabis can be bought and sold legally, albeit on a small and well-controlled scale. It remains to be seen how well this approach works. Furthermore, Holland has recently tightened up its drugs laws in line with recent EU legislation.

'I started out drinking with my mates. We used to drink, then go around smashing up bars and cars. Now we smoke dope, we want to be sociable and chat to girls. It gives you that cool, positive way of thinking.'
(A cannabis user)

In 1991, a report in the science magazine *Nature* put forward the suggestion that smoking cannabis might help people see in the dark.

> **'If cannabis were legalised, it would stop it being trendy, then no one would want to smoke it anyway.'**
> *(A parent)*

At present, however, it is a criminal act to possess or supply cannabis. Thinking it should be legalised will not do anything to help your case if you are caught.

Dealing? There are quite a lot of people involved, a wide network. There are the importers — there are blocks of them. You've got a kind of hierarchy: the top person knows a few people, sells it to his friends and maybe keeps the best for himself.

The longer you smoke hash, the more you get to know people. You can work your way up from a small scale, like, say, you buy an ounce of resin for £80–£90 and then you sell eighths for £15 ... that's £120. These might be college students or unemployed kids. You can drift into supplying from there: you can see who's the key person in the group. So you end up with one person who you know, who can supply, at the cheapest rate, good quality and a fair weight.

So you've built up a regular supply, and regular customers. Once people know you smoke, they'll often come up to you and ask you. You can get a vastly overblown reputation. Everyone always wants to know your contact – they want to take on the same role. Some will just always depend on me to get them stuff.

Dealers aren't amazingly friendly ... they don't want to get people hanging around with them – they don't want to draw attention to themselves. They want to deal as quickly as possible and move on. There isn't really a rivalry, they know and talk to each other – but they will sometimes back-stab the others.

Where they deal depends on whether they have a flat to themselves: I know a few who have a flat – so they get away from street dealing.

You get customers through word of mouth. You can tell by the look of them who does drugs and who doesn't: it's almost like a hidden language. Roaching rollies (using home-rolled cigarettes with a cardboard filter) is a certain giveaway.

There's a certain amount of paranoia if you're dealing. There was one time when we were at home, sitting around smoking, when I thought I saw flashing lights outside – so I went out to bury the gear in the garden. Then later, when I realised it was OK, I went out and couldn't find it! It took an hour, digging about in the dark, with a torch, before I could find it again.

And some friends, they had a big plastic bag full of weed, and were driving down the main road and saw a police car behind them, so Alan, who was driving, said 'For God's sake, get rid of it!' So they started chucking bits out of the window. Then they'd lost the police car, so they were cursing – then they saw it again, so they started chucking more out. There was Alan, saying 'Chuck it!' and Rob and Pete saying, 'No, don't waste it' – and in the end, there was hardly any left.

Another time we were in Adam's flat, and he had an eighth. Someone said there were lots of police about. Well, getting stoned makes you feel a bit paranoid – it's difficult to hide the fact that you're stoned. This time, Adam got so paranoid (and it wasn't even enough to be *really worried about) that he hid everything, he wouldn't smoke any more; he hid it all behind this tile by the fireplace. He kept getting it out, then he'd put it away again.*

Adam did try to deal a bit – but then he smokes it all himself, he can't bear not to smoke it. He'd get a bit to sell, and then take a bit off it and a bit off it, till it was not even enough to sell.

My brother Joe, he got done for dealing. He'd been dealing for some time, then when he went to university, they caught him. There's a lot of talk and gossip on the campus, and that's obviously how they found out. They were waiting in his room for him to come back. That's what sometimes happens – it tends to be a knock on the door, or they're waiting outside your house, and get you as you're about to go in. He got two months for 'possession with intent to supply' – that's reasonable, it was the first time he'd been caught. The two months ran so that he only missed a week or so of the next term. But we all felt pretty bad about it – my mum especially.
(Jake, 19)

DRUG-RELATED CRIME

'Drugs bring their very own built-in crime wave with them.'
(A police officer)

We've talked about how drug taking can lead to crime, in order for users to get the money together to fund their habit. Many users shoplift and steal goods, then sell them for far less than they are worth in order to make money

108

quickly. Some steal money and jewellery from their parents or friends; some burgle other people's houses. Either way, they're really asking for trouble.

'One crack user admitted to 1,000 crimes.'
(A police officer)

Chapter 4

DRUGS

DRUGS AROUND
THE CORNER

So far, we've looked at drugs which, despite the occasional murmurs about legalising cannabis, are strictly illegal to possess, buy or sell. But these are not the only drugs you'll come across. There are some you might not think of as drugs at all. These are the so-called legal drugs. A harmless enough cup of tea or coffee contains the stimulant drug, caffeine. The paracetamol you take for headaches is a drug, as are cold cures and cough mixtures.

And, of course, there's tobacco and alcohol, two of the most lethal legal drugs around. But they are very much part of people's social lives, so they are seen (perhaps wrongly) as much less dangerous than drugs such as heroin or cocaine. Are there double standards at work? Yes! People who quite happily, and regularly, have a drink at home or in the pub, would be appalled if their son or daughter were caught smoking a joint. And yet alcohol and tobacco are highly addictive drugs, whereas cannabis is not. And alcohol and tobacco kill more people each year than heroin and cocaine put together and doubled.

'There's a different set of values attached to tobacco and alcohol which just makes them more dangerous.'
(A teacher)

THE MEDICINES ACT

The manufacture and supply of medical drugs is controlled by law, more specifically by the Medicines Act 1968. It divides medicines up into three groups. 'Prescription only' drugs can only be supplied by a qualified and registered chemist, and only if they have been prescribed by a doctor.

The second group can be sold without a prescription, but only by a qualified chemist. The third group of drugs can be sold in any shop, not just a chemist's: no prescription is needed.

PRESCRIPTION DRUGS

'Serious drug users used to think nothing of stealing prescription pads from doctors' surgeries, or of breaking in and stealing the drugs themselves.'
(A GP)

Tranquillisers and barbiturates are, according to the Medicines Act, 'prescription only' drugs. Doctors prescribe them for medical purposes but they are often misused. Here's a bit more about them.

Tranquillisers

The history

Doctors prescribe minor tranquillisers such as Temazepam, Valium and Librium to people who have difficulty sleeping or who are extremely anxious or worried about something. They are the most commonly prescribed drugs in Britain. Over 20 million tranquilliser prescriptions are given out each year. Tranquillisers are not illegal if they are prescribed for you; they are illegal, if they are not. However, recent changes in the law have made Temazepam (an increasingly misused drug) harder to obtain by encouraging GPs to prescribe less harmful drugs.

In appearance

These drugs are made as powders and then formed into tablets and capsules.

Taking tranquillisers

Tranquillisers are usually taken by mouth. Temazepam, though supplied in capsules containing a liquid or gel, is often injected by drug users. This causes extreme intoxication and agitation, and has caused many deaths, because the liquid or jelly from the capsules has blocked the veins when injected.

The effects

Tranquillisers depress mental activity; they have a calming, relaxing effect and relieve worry and tension. They can also help people to sleep. Some drug users take tranquillisers to calm them down after taking amphetamines or Ecstasy, or to increase the effects of heroin.

Dangers, side-effects, overload

One of the main problems with tranquillisers is that people can become dependent on them. If users stop taking them, they can suffer quite severe withdrawal symptoms such as irritability, sleeplessness, anxiety, vomiting and even fits. Many people carry on taking tranquillisers long after their original problems are cured, because they find it too difficult to do without them.

Valium is frequently mixed with alcohol, which is a very dangerous practice, as it causes the user to lose consciousness and sometimes to vomit and choke. Other dangers include blocked veins, which can be fatal; the risk of overdosing; and accidents due to extreme 'drunkenness'.

Aka (also known as)

Tranx **greenies jellies**
mazzies happies *dizzies*
eggs **pams** *downers*

'I tried giving them up but I couldn't cope so I started again. Now I can't get through the day without them.'
(A tranquilliser user)

Barbiturates

The history
Barbiturates are only rarely prescribed medically, to help people with severe sleep problems and in the control of serious epilepsy. They are 'Prescription only' drugs under the Medicines Act. THEY ARE ALSO CLASS B DRUGS UNDER THE MISUSE OF DRUGS ACT. They are not illegal if they have been prescribed for you, but they are illegal if they haven't been. Barbiturates are often misused.

In appearance
They are made as powders, and formed into either tablets or, more often, into coloured capsules.

Taking barbiturates
They are usually taken by mouth. Some misusers inject them – a very dangerous thing to do (see pages 46 for more

about the risks involved in injecting drugs). There is a high risk of overdose or infection if you inject barbiturates. Barbiturates for non-medical use are usually stolen or obtained (legally) by prescription and passed on (illegally) to someone else.

The effects

Barbiturates are depressants ('downers') which depress the nervous system. A small dose can make people feel relaxed and happy, as if they've had a couple of alcoholic drinks.

Dangers, side-effects, overload

Larger doses of barbiturates can make people feel depressed, worried, clumsy and confused. It is easy to overdose with barbiturates, resulting in breathing failure and death. If you've been drinking, you may only need half the usual dose to overdose and die. Long-term use can lead to people becoming dependent on the drugs. There's also a risk of fits or even death if you come off barbiturates too quickly. (Phenobarbitone, an anti-epilepsy drug, is often combined with heroin without the buyer knowing. Since coming off barbiturates can cause fits, this may come as an unpleasant surprise to heroin users trying to kick their habit.)

Aka (also known as)

(OTC (over the counter) Drugs)

These are a group of medicines which you can buy from

the chemist's quite legally, without a prescription, but which can be and frequently are misused. (The chemist may refuse to sell them to you, however, if he or she thinks there is a chance of misuse.) They include cough mixtures and cold cures, which contain drugs such as codeine (an opiate, see pages 59-60). Drug users sometimes turn to OTC drugs if their supplies of drugs or of cash are running low. Here are just a few OTC drugs you might have come across.

Cough Linctuses and Cold Cures

Some cough linctuses contain small amounts of the opiate codeine, a highly addictive drug. This is converted into morphine inside your body. If you really have a cough and take the prescribed dose of the linctus, you may feel better. It's when the drug is misused that the problems arise. Some cold cures and decongestants contain drugs to dry up a runny nose. One such drug is the stimulant ephedrine. Some cold cures also contain paracetamol (see below).

Paracetamol

Paracetamol is an analgesic (pain killer) which is taken in tablet form to cure headaches and other aches and pains. A paracetamol pill looks pretty harmless but if you take too many tablets, or too large a dose of cold cures containing paracetamol, you could overdose and suffer irreparable liver damage and even death.

ALWAYS FOLLOW THE INSTRUCTIONS ON THE PACKET – even something which looks as harmless as paracetamol can kill.

'I'm always having rows with my mum and dad: it's usually about what I wear, or how often I'm going out and staying out late – like, I shouldn't stay out late on weekdays and things like that. Sometimes I feel they just don't remember what it's like to be young. I mean, my dad used to get really angry about me wearing short skirts, and say, 'You're not going out looking like that, are you?' or make comments about my boyfriend, say he was too old for me or whatever – and sometimes I'd get upset, or rush back up to my room and slam the door ... but now I just shout, 'I'm going out. Bye!' and go before they can say anything.

Well, this weekend I got in really late on the Friday, and there was an almighty row, and they grounded me, said I couldn't go out Saturday night. I had to go into town Saturday morning, and then I just went round my friend's and didn't go home. I was supposed to be meeting my boyfriend, and couldn't just not go, could I? So I did go and meet him, but it ended up with us having a row because he was chatting up another girl, and he dumped me.

So then I had to go home and face another row with my parents, which I really didn't need just then. I went upstairs feeling really miserable and just lay on the bed, and after a bit I went into the bathroom and got a load of paracetamol out of the medicine cabinet and swallowed them down. I suppose I didn't really think what could happen, I just felt so rotten.

I lay on my bed thinking, Well, they don't care, they're all right ... and then after about an hour I felt a bit dizzy, and sick, but I couldn't be sick – and I thought Oh, my god, what have I done? I might be going to die. I wished I hadn't done it, honestly. In the end I went and told my mum, and then they rang the doctor and rushed me into hospital, to the Casualty department. I had to have my stomach washed out:

119

they put a rubber hose down your throat and it makes you sick and – it was horrible.

After we got home again, once I was all right, we had a talk about it all. My mum was ever so upset – she said I could have died, because it doesn't take many paracetamol at all to do serious damage to your liver, and that can kill you. It's a good job I told them in time. I suppose it was everything going wrong at once, and I felt I couldn't do anything right. But I know now the rows were really because they don't want me to get hurt, I suppose because they love me, really. It helped that we talked about it. I felt quite stupid afterwards.
(Nicky, 14)

Antihistamines

Antihistamines are used medically to treat allergic reactions, such as hay fever and rashes caused by insect bites or stings. They work by neutralising the body's histamines (substances released by the body in allergic reactions) which cause irritation. They are also found in some cough and cold medicines and can be used to treat travel sickness. If they are used properly, they bring welcome relief. However, some antihistamines cause drowsiness and loss of co-ordination, which can be dangerous. It is even more serious if you mix the drugs with alcohol. Antihistamines are sometimes taken by opiate users to stop them feeling sick, or may even be mixed with heroin or methadone – a dangerous cocktail. Heavy abuse of antihistamines can cause brain damage, violent behaviour and fits.

TOBACCO

'I had my first cigarette when I was about 16. We were doing exams and I was really tense. Lots of people smoked and someone offered me one. I didn't feel sick or dizzy or anything, so I just carried on smoking. It wasn't hard.'
(18-year-old smoker)

'My parents smoked so I was used to people smoking. It didn't seem like a big deal.'
(17-year-old smoker)

'I really panic as I start to run out.'
(17-year-old smoker)

IN BRITAIN, SMOKING KILLS ONE PERSON EVERY FIVE MINUTES.

WHY DO PEOPLE SMOKE?

Here's what some young smokers had to say about it:

It's cool to smoke

It was bored

It's sociable

All my friends were doing it

It keeps you thin

I just wanted to see what it was like

It calms me down if I'm stressed out

It makes me feel more confident

My parents didn't want me to, so I did!

Now I can't stop

My friend gave me one. I liked it so I carried on

These are just some of the reasons why people smoke. At the time, you don't think that it will do you any harm. After all, plenty of people smoke, including perhaps your parents and teachers, so why shouldn't you? Even though you know all about the effects on your health, you never think any of them could happen to you. But if you try a cigarette, for whatever reason, and you like the taste and smell, you'll probably have another and another. Pretty soon, you find that you crave cigarettes more and more often, and can't go for very long without one. This is because the nicotine in tobacco is one of the most highly addictive drugs known. It's even more addictive than heroin.

'The thing is, it's a habit now. I've tried giving up but when you really crave a cigarette, having one seems like the answer to all your problems. I'd like to give up, I mean I know it's not good for me, but I'm too scared.'
(18-year-old smoker)

Whatever your reasons for starting, **SMOKING WILL DAMAGE YOUR HEALTH AND MAY EVEN KILL YOU.**

Tobacco and the law

It is not illegal to possess, buy or smoke tobacco but it is against the law for shopkeepers to sell tobacco to young people under the age of 16. It is also breaking the law to smoke in non-smoking zones on buses, trains, in cafés and so on, and you can be fined for doing so.

In 17th-century Russia, the penalty for smoking was extremely harsh. Tsar Michael hated smoking so much he decreed that first offenders should have the soles of their feet beaten with a stick, second-time offenders should have their noses slit and third-time offenders should be put to death!

What's in tobacco?

Nicotine This is a stimulant which takes only seven seconds to reach your brain. (This is what makes many first-time smokers feel dizzy.) It is a highly poisonous and addictive chemical.

Tar Tar is one of the main cancer-causing ingredients in tobacco. It is a sticky brown substance which collects in your lungs and air passages and clogs them up. It stains your teeth, tongue and fingers yellow.

Carbon monoxide This is a deadly gas, produced by the process of burning tobacco, which enters your bloodstream when you smoke and stops your circulation system working properly. New cars are fitted with devices to cut down carbon monoxide emissions in their exhaust fumes. New smokers *choose* to breathe this in!

'I always admired the people who smoked. It was daring and cool. It made me feel part of their group. I felt really proud of myself, actually.'
  (18-year-old smoker)

WHAT HAPPENS WHEN YOU SMOKE?

The facts:
● About a quarter of 15-year-olds smoke at least one cigarette a week. Some start smoking as young as nine or ten years old. In total, about 40 per cent of adults are smokers.

● Almost two thirds of young smokers say that they want to stop.

● On average, for every cigarette smoked, a smoker loses five and a half minutes of his or her life.

● Over four times as many premature deaths are caused by smoking as by road accidents, alcohol, drug abuse, suicide and all other avoidable risks put together.

● Nicotine is a deadly poison. In an experiment, a drop of pure nicotine placed on a rabbit's skin killed the rabbit in ten seconds.

When you smoke, you draw into your lungs a cocktail of about 400 different chemicals. Nicotine is just one of these chemicals. It is a stimulant, which perks you up. It is also the chemical responsible for getting you addicted to cigarettes. But other chemicals, including tar and carbon monoxide, can cause cancer, irritate your airways, cause serious breathing problems, and carry a risk of thrombosis (blood clotting), particularly in women who take the pill. The hot air that smokers inhale is a major cause of cancer and bronchitis, because it dries and irritates the lining of the lungs, mouth and windpipe.

IN THE SHORT TERM

You might think you look really cool when you smoke. The reality is rather different:

● Your breath smells of smoke.

● Your hair and clothes smell of smoke (you might not notice, because smoking also affects people's sense of smell and of taste).

● You are more prone to hacking coughs.

● Your teeth and fingers are stained yellow.

● It's a very expensive habit to support.

IN THE LONG TERM

Smoker's cough

Cigarette smoke makes it more difficult for your lungs to

work. The insides of your windpipe and the tubes leading into your lungs (called the bronchi) are lined with millions of tiny hairs, called cilia, coated with slimy mucus. These keep your lungs dirt, germ and disease free. The chemicals in cigarette smoke stop the cilia working properly. Mucus collects in your airways and you have to cough to clear it. This is how you get so-called 'smoker's cough'.

In general, smokers are more likely to suffer from chesty coughs, asthma and shortness of breath than non-smokers.

Lung cancer

The tar in cigarette smoke and the irritant hot air damages the delicate tissue of your lungs and can cause lung cancer. This prevents the lungs from working properly and makes breathing very difficult and painful. Cancer is a disease which can easily spread to other parts of the body. Nine out of ten people with lung cancer are dead within five years of finding out they have the disease.

Smoking can also contribute to cancers of the throat, lips and the neck of the womb, and can harm unborn babies.

'Half of all serious smokers die of the habit. Smokers are three times more likely to die in middle age than non-smokers.'
(Imperial Cancer Research Fund survey)

Bronchitis and emphysema

Bronchitis is the inflammation of the bronchi, which become swollen with mucus. Emphysema happens when the fine, spongy material in the lungs, the alveoli, gets damaged and cannot work properly. Both these diseases leave the sufferer painfully gasping for breath.

Heart disease

Smoking is one of the main causes of heart disease. Cigarette smoke damages the coronary arteries, the blood vessels which carry blood to the muscles of the heart. It can weaken the vessel walls and cause fatty deposits to build up in them, making them too narrow to carry enough blood to the heart. The heart cannot work properly and before you know it, you've had a heart attack. This can also happen if a clot of blood blocks one of the blood vessels and your heart stops beating. Smoking makes blood stickier than normal and more likely to clot. Some people recover from heart attacks; others don't.

Sometimes the arteries in smokers' legs and arms become blocked, preventing blood circulating properly round the body. Doctors often have no choice but to amputate the affected limbs.

Stopping smoking

After only one year without smoking the extra risk of heart disease is reduced by half. After 15 years, ex-smokers have almost the same risks as people who have never smoked.

Eleven million people in Britain have given up smoking and stayed off cigarettes.

The good news is that you can stop smoking and reverse the health hazards before it's too late. If you want to give up, here are some hints to help you:

1. First of all, decide that you want to, and are going to, stop. Willpower is all-important.

2. Write a list of all the benefits of giving up smoking – feeling fitter, smelling less like an ashtray, being able to taste your food again and saving lots of money.

3. Fix a day for giving up. Tell as many people as possible that you are going to stop on that day.

4. Find something to fiddle with – a small pebble or some worry beads or a biro. It will stop your hands feeling empty without a cigarette.

5. Throw away any ashtrays and paraphernalia associated with smoking (lighters, matchboxes etc).

6. Now STOP SMOKING! If you really crave a fag, take a couple of deep breaths, eat a piece of fruit, or go for a walk.

7. Put the money you've saved each day into a jar. When you've got enough, buy yourself something really luxurious.

If you find giving up too difficult the first time, try again. Most people give up several times before they finally succeed. There are various things around to help you – like nicotine chewing gum, nicotine patches and so on. Your doctor or chemist will know all about them.

> **'One of the reasons I gave up was because there were so few places where you could smoke any more. I got sick of the dirty looks and the feeling of panic when I couldn't find somewhere to smoke. Giving up was hell but at least I'm free to come and go as I please now.'**
> *(An ex-smoker)*

Withdrawal symptoms

When you stop smoking, you are actually withdrawing from a very powerfully addictive drug. It takes time to clear the drug from your system and to break the habit. You might feel constantly hungry, have a hacking cough, not be able to sleep, have strange dreams, find it hard to concentrate, feel light-headed, depressed or tearful and get very bad tempered. These symptoms will all disappear in a few weeks. You might still crave cigarettes, that's the habit part, and find you feel lost without a cigarette in your hand. Give it time – and feel really proud of yourself when you succeed.

Passive smoking

If you smoke, it's not only your health that you're putting at risk. A lot of research has been done into the dangers of 'passive smoking', that is, breathing in other people's cigarette smoke. And it has been found that passive smoking can cause lung cancer in non-smokers – for example, young children. There are other health effects – allergies, asthma and headaches. Passive smoking may also increase the risk of heart disease in non-smokers. Hardly fair, is it? There are also the problems of other people's smoke making your clothes smell, your eyes run and making you cough.

I don't ever want to smoke – my Mum smokes, and I hate it. She tells us, 'Don't you ever start smoking!' We say to her, 'But you smoke, Mum,' and she goes, 'Yeah, but look how hard I've tried to give it up.'

She started smoking when she was ten, and when she met my Dad she was smoking sixty a day. She says she cut it down a lot when she was pregnant with us: she went to see the midwife, because she was trying to give up altogether, and couldn't, and she got so het up about it all that the midwife said, 'If you're down to just four a day, it's best to leave it at that, rather than get yourself in such a state trying to give up altogether.' But then, she went back to smoking after we were born.

Oh, the number of times she's tried to give up – I've lost count. One time she went to a hypnotist: that was when she was on sixty a day, and she managed to give up for six weeks, then she went back, but only to twenty a day. She's been on twenty a day for ages, on and off. Once she tried to give up, without any special method, just giving up – but she says it was a nightmare. She was edgy, and bad-tempered with us and with Dad, and that didn't last long! The last time, she nearly succeeded. She used those nicotine patches: they cost a fortune. She got on really well, she'd given up – at least, stopped smoking; but the patches, they give you nicotine through the skin, don't they? The dose gets weaker and weaker, and when she got to the last one, the weakest, she couldn't keep it up. She just had to have a cigarette. And then after that, it was back to smoking again. It just shows, doesn't it, how your body gets addicted?

My younger brother and sister, they say, 'You're on drugs, Mum,' but I know that cigarettes are different: they're legal drugs, so it's not the same. I don't like it, though. I hate the smell. Well, Mum hates it, too – that's the funny thing. She drums it into us, not even to try one or two; she says you can get addicted after only a few cigarettes. You really crave the nicotine. And she says it can damage your brain cells, as well as give you lung cancer. I just don't even want to start. I wish Mum could give up, though.
(Daniel, 12)

ALCOHOL

More than 90 per cent of adults in Britain drink to some extent. Young people in their late teens seem to drink more than average. A third of young people aged between 13-16 drink once a week, usually at home.
(A recent survey)

'I felt really sick after I'd had my first drink and I vowed I'd never drink again. But I did.'
(15-year-old)

'I go for a drink with my friends every Friday because it's the end of the week and you can relax. If I'm in the mood, drinking makes me really happy and giggly. If I'm not, it just makes me fed up.'
(18-year-old)

Alcohol is a very powerful drug. Its misuse kills over 33,000 people a year.

WHAT'S ALL THE FUSS ABOUT?

People have made and drunk alcohol for thousands of years, and alcohol is certainly part of everyday life in our society. You may drink to be sociable, to relax or because you like it, and there doesn't seem to be any harm in that. But alcohol is a powerful and potentially addictive drug, and you need to be aware of its effects, especially if you misuse it.

IN THE SHORT TERM

When you drink, the alcohol is absorbed into your bloodstream. It takes about five to ten minutes to take effect, but the effects can last for several hours. Of course, how alcohol affects you depends on how much you have drunk, how quickly you've drunk it, how strong it is (spirits are stronger than beer, for example) and whether you've had anything to eat beforehand (a good move, if you don't want to risk a hangover).

And the effects? Well, as you probably know, alcohol can make you feel great – relaxed, confident, etc. It can also make you feel terrible: sick, dizzy, headachy, clumsy. It's a bit of a myth that alcohol cheers people up – it is actually a depressant and you may end up crying into your drink rather than having a laugh.

> **'I didn't think I was drunk. But I couldn't stop my words slurring, and, when I stood up, the room started spinning round. I felt (and I was) really, really sick.'**
> *(16-year-old)*

Because alcohol reduces people's self control, there's a real danger of their hurting themselves or other people (by accident or on purpose!). There's the risk of drinking too much, falling asleep and choking on their own vomit. Then there's the hangover – waking up and knowing that if you move your head will split open, but you have to get up and go to school or work.

NEVER MIX ALCOHOL WITH OTHER DRUGS – IT CAN BE FATAL.

IN THE LONG TERM

If you're healthy anyway, and if you drink in moderation

(i.e. at most a couple of drinks a day), you shouldn't have a long-term problem with alcohol. But if you drink heavily over a long period (the figures given for heavy drinking are 5-7 pints of beer, or the equivalent, a day for men and 3-5 pints a day for women), you run the risk of brain damage, liver disease (called cirrhosis), mouth and throat cancer, heart problems and stomach ulcers. Most of these can be fatal.

People often forget that alcohol is full of calories, hence the 'beer gut' of heavy beer drinkers. One pint of beer contains about 180 calories.

Alcohol can be addictive and you can become dependent on it. Several hundred thousand people in Britain are thought to be alcoholics. Some of them are not much older than you.

WHY DO PEOPLE DRINK?

Here are some reasons given by a group of 15-year-olds:

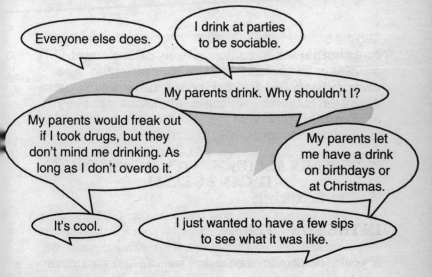

Everyone else does.

I drink at parties to be sociable.

My parents drink. Why shouldn't I?

My parents would freak out if I took drugs, but they don't mind me drinking. As long as I don't overdo it.

My parents let me have a drink on birthdays or at Christmas.

It's cool.

I just wanted to have a few sips to see what it was like.

ALCOHOL AND THE LAW

It is against the law for alcohol to be sold to people under 18 years old, although it is not illegal for you to drink if you are not yet 18. (It is, however, illegal to give alcohol to children under five.) Shopkeepers do have the right to refuse to sell you alcohol if they think you look too young, even if you're not.

Alcohol can only be sold on licensed premises, such as pubs (where it can be drunk on the premises) and 'off-licences' (where it can't be). There are special laws dictating the opening hours of pubs and off-licences.

It is an offence to be drunk and disorderly and you can be arrested for it.

It is against the law to drive if you have had too much to drink. NEVER drink and drive – the risks of causing death or injury to yourself or others are simply not worth taking.

> 'Alcohol is a major cause of accidents. More than half of the people who are breathalysed by the police have twice as much alcohol in their systems as they should have.'
> (Health Education Authority)

Safer drinking

If you are worried about how much you are drinking, there are various ways of keeping check on yourself. Keep count of how many units of alcohol you are drinking. Spread over a week, (i.e. not all in one night!) the safe limits are usually given as 21 units for men and 14 units for women although recent recommendations have suggested that this should be increased to 28 for men and 21 for women.

1 unit = 1/2 pint beer, lager or cider (this means normal strength beer, lager or cider; not the extra-strong stuff. There is much less of that per unit.)

1 unit = 1 standard glass of wine

1 unit = 1 single measure of spirits (gin, whisky, vodka etc)

1 unit = 1 small glass of sherry

You may also have a problem with drink if you:

● drink heavily when you're under stress or depressed;

● drink on your own, rather than with other people;

● try but fail to drink less;

● drink in the morning before you go to school;

● lie about how much you drink and when you drink;

● find that drinking affects your memory and your performance at school (you may start getting low marks when you've always had good marks before, etc);

● become violent when you've been drinking;

● get the shakes and feel terrible when you give up.

If you think you have a problem with drinking, there are some contact addresses and telephone numbers at the back of the book where you can get help and advice.

> If you drink at all, you are affected by alcohol. The more you drink and the more often you drink, the greater the risks to your health.

> Young and old people are affected more quickly by alcohol and are consequently more at risk.

So, get wise and stay in control. There's not much point having a really great time but feeling like death warmed up afterwards and not being able to remember it, is there?

My mum had a problem with alcohol – well, she was an alcoholic, to be honest. It goes back almost as far as I can remember. My dad had left when I was quite little, she had three kids and no money – so I suppose that was why she turned to drink. But we saw that as normal. When I started going to school, everything seemed OK, but then a few months later, things got a bit weird. We'd be upstairs, gone to bed, and I'd come down for a snack in the middle of the night, and Mum would be there watching the telly with a couple of cans. Then after a bit it must have been quite a bit more ... I didn't really understand what it meant, being drunk. I'd turn to my older brother and say, 'Mum's turned funny again.' He was the one who explained it to me. Jack was like the man about the house, holding it all together: he'd cook, and look after everyone.

She'd be fine for a few days, and then she'd have a bout of constant drinking. She'd get us up, we'd go off to school, and when we got home she'd be in bed asleep, or lying by the phone or something – I suppose she'd been trying to phone the doctor. Sometimes she'd get the tea, and go off upstairs while we were eating; or my brother would get the tea and I'd look after my little sister. Sometimes she'd go out to the pub and not come back for a long time. She always did come home in the end, and then she'd send us to the pub for some food, nuts and crisps. We used to worry about her coming home blind drunk – my brother sometimes went to the pub with her, to bring her home. But when she was sober, she was fine, like a rock – and she'd cook lovely meals, filling stews and things.

It got to the stage, though, that we couldn't let her go upstairs on her own, because she might fall down. It was always Jack who'd ring for the ambulance, and my sister and I'd be holding her head, or the pillow – and there'd be alarms, and people rushing about, and Anna with big, wide eyes, not knowing what was going on. One time, she had to have twenty-seven stitches. People in the village knew what was going on: sometimes a neighbour would look after us if Mum was at the hospital.

It was quite tough at school: we didn't tell anyone, but money was short, and we didn't have the expensive football boots or Star Wars toys that other kids had – they used to laugh at us. We just had to say, 'We haven't any money.' The teachers were concerned, you could tell, when everyone else's parents turned up at parents' evenings, and ours didn't – but we'd just say, 'No, everything's fine.' We didn't dare to tell: we didn't know what would happen. I was scared by that. I was scared of the situation, not of Mum.

Occasionally they'd take her into hospital for detox and rehabilitation – sometimes she'd admit herself, and sign herself out again when she was ready. Those times, we'd go to volunteers who'd look after us for a while until she was sober. But in the end, the social services stepped in and we were taken into care. That was horrible: I'd want to visit her, because it was only the next village; I'd say, 'Can't I go and see Mum?' and they'd say, 'No, it's not a good idea' – we only saw her for a couple of hours at weekends. I'd get so angry; I'd say, 'If she can't see us, she'll get worse' – but they were so sure they knew best. And because we'd been taken away, she was really making an effort.

There were several years of this: us living with foster parents, which wasn't always a very happy experience – at one point my brother and I slept rough for a while – then at my dad's, then back with Mum... I know Mum felt bad about it, and she tried really hard: she'd make a real effort, and then things would go to pot again. But now, at last, she's had no alcohol for over a year. She realised no one else was helping her, the only one who could help was herself. It's been bloody hard, but she's done it.

I know there were things in Mum's life that made her turn to alcohol. I'd say to anyone who turns to drinking in order to forget, That's not the way. Alcohol just causes more problems. I know there were times when Mum stole, even – she needed clothes and food for us, as well as drink – but even when things were bad, she always put us first. And now we can talk about it, and I can say to her, 'Look it wasn't your fault. It was the situation.' But alcohol really is a poison; it messes with your head.

(Mark, 19)

Chapter 5

DRUGS

HELP!

Whether you are a drug user yourself and want to give up, or you know someone – a friend or a relative – who you think may be using drugs and having problems, don't worry – HELP IS AT HAND. Drugs are such a tricky subject, it's often difficult to think clearly about how and where to get help. People's emotions and fears all too often get in the way of practical advice and action. And the whole business of getting treatment for a drugs problem can seem very frightening and confusing. Don't worry – there are plenty of places you can go to for information, advice and counselling. And if they can't help with a specific problem, they'll put you in touch with someone who can. You will find lots of useful addresses and telephone numbers at the back of this book, on pages 175-185.

KICKING THE HABIT

There are lots of reasons for wanting to give up drugs, just as there are lots of reasons why people turn to them in the first place. If you have used drugs for a while, you might have lost touch with your friends and family because they don't like what drugs are doing to you and don't understand the problem. You might be fed up with feeling terrible most of the time, with the occasional high, and with feeling guilty, or depressed, or out of control. Regaining your health and self-esteem is an important part of giving up drugs.

Whatever the reasons, there are a couple of things to remember:

- It's not going to be easy.

- It'll be worth it in the end.

Wherever you live in Britain, there are places you can go to for help, once you've decided you need it. If you can't talk to your parents, try your friends. If they can't help, you could try your doctor or a teacher, if you have a good enough relationship with them. Otherwise, there are *confidential helplines* you can phone who will give you the numbers and addresses of local drug counselling and advisory services in your area. (See the back of the book for some helpline numbers.) *All these services are confidential – they want to help you, not to get you into any more trouble.* If you are really desperate, try phoning the Samaritans (number in the phone book) – they will be able to put you in touch with more specialist helpers. If you have been taking drugs and feel very ill, you can go to the casualty department of your local hospital for treatment.

> **'Most of our new clients refer themselves to us for counselling.'**
> *(Drug counselling service)*

In a recent survey, three quarters of those asked said they would talk to their friends if they had a drugs problem; only a very few said they'd talk to their parents; slightly more said they'd talk to a doctor or nurse.

IN THE LONGER TERM

'Most drug users do actually want help but they are frightened or unsure about getting it.'
(Drugs counsellor)

Many towns have their own local community drugs services which offer information, counselling and advice. They work with local doctors, social workers and the police. They may also run needle-exchange schemes (see page 95) and can organise home visits and refer the people they see to residential centres if necessary. Many of these community services are staffed mainly by trained volunteers. They also have teams of doctors, therapists and even lawyers to offer advice. They can organise tests for HIV and hepatitis, and offer counselling for friends and relatives of drug users.

Some serious drug users can be helped at home, by their family, with regular visits to (and support from) a drugs counsellor. It may be a good idea to have a kind of contract, about what people expect from each other, in order to co-operate – perhaps with certain privileges as incentives, to encourage the user to give up. Sometimes it can be very hard for the family: they may have to be quite tough in order to help. There are times when it may seem an uphill struggle (on both sides) so it is important to have advisers to give extra support when necessary – and to remind you: *DON'T GIVE UP. It's worth it.* It's also good to have someone to remind you that you have a right to feel really pleased with yourself when you've successfully given up.

People who have used drugs such as heroin or alcohol for a long time and are heavily addicted to them may be able to have treatment in a special residential centre. Here they are gradually weaned off the drug, under careful medical supervision. They cannot avoid physical withdrawal symptoms but these may be no worse than a bad bout of flu and will disappear after ten days or so. The psychological craving for a drug may last much longer, and staying off the drug, once the treatment is over, can be extremely difficult. It's more likely to be successful if you have the backing and encouragement of your family and friends. It can be all too easy to return to drugs if something goes wrong and you have no one to support you.

There is a relatively small number of places in residential centres, however, and with local authorities constantly short of money, this is not likely to increase in the near future. So only a small minority of drug users ever get to a residential centre, and only a minority of those successfully complete the course or maintain a drug-free lifestyle after leaving. Most addicts will find help with local community teams: for example, the vast majority of heroin addicts are either maintained (held on a legal prescription) or weaned off using methadone in the community with the aid of a local drug service or GP.

However they are helped, for most people coming off drugs is a slow process of learning to live life without drugs and may involve many failures, before they finally free themselves of their habit.

'Most community drugs teams find that if a person stays in the area they have moved to, they stand a reasonable chance of succeeding. If they return to their former community it is rare for them to maintain a controlled lifestyle without a great deal of additional help.'
(A drugs advisor)

'A couple of us were trying to help a friend though "cold turkey". I went to stay the night, and was to keep an eye on Marie during the day. The next day, there was something I'd forgotten to do, so I had to go out for about half an hour. When I came back, Marie was gone. I was frantic. She came back about two hours later, saying she'd just had to go out and sign on. I breathed a huge sigh of relief. A couple of days later, she admitted that she'd actually gone off to her dealer, and bought enough heroin to get her through the next two or three days. I felt such a fool. I knew so little about the drug, I couldn't tell if she was on or off it, and she knew she could wind me round her little finger.'
(Friend of a drug user)

TELL-TALE SIGNS AND SIGNALS

If you think someone you know has a drug problem, there are quite a few warning signs and clues which you can look out for. But it's not easy to be sure. For a start, people take drugs for a variety of reasons and are affected by different drugs in different ways. You might be looking for changes in their behaviour, but they won't necessarily be the same changes in everyone. Some people may seem very up; others very down. Whatever you do, don't start suspecting everyone you know of being a drug user. Some of your friends may just be going through a difficult time – it may have nothing whatsoever to do with drugs!

Signs of drug use
There are some general signs to watch out for which may be linked to drug use:

- sudden changes of mood from happy and cheerful to fed up and sullen;

- loss of appetite and loss of weight;

- feeling tired all the time;

- uncharacteristic fits of temper;

- becoming withdrawn and uncommunicative;

- playing truant from school;

- mixing with an older crowd;

- losing interest in previous set of friends or in hobbies or sport;

- taking no care of personal appearance;

- wearing sunglasses at odd times of the day to hide red eyes or dilated (large) or constricted (small) pupils;

- using perfume, incense or aftershave to hide the smell of drugs;

- using slang associated with drugs;

- always being broke and trying to borrow money;

- large plastic drinks bottles with the base removed;

- bent bits of piping;

- lots of matches and/or cigarette lighters;

- packets of cigarette papers with pieces torn from them to make roaches;

- buckets or bowls of water.

But don't jump to conclusions straight away – you may be wrong.

There are more specific signs to look out for with the invidual types of drugs, and various pieces of equipment associated with them. For example:

Amphetamines

Signs: greater amount of energy; sleeplessness; loss of appetite; may become aggressive; paranoia.

Clues: wraps of paper which the drug is sold in; white, pink or yellow traces of powder; tablets; needles and syringes (if injecting amphetamines).

Cannabis

Signs: red eyes, dilated pupils; lack of co-ordination; giggliness for no reason.

Clues: strong, sickly sweet cannabis smell, or the smell of incense sticks used to hide it; butts of joints (see page 29) with cardboard filters; packets of cigarette rolling paper.

Cocaine

Signs: more alert and excitable; dilated pupils; light hurts eyes; feeling depressed; faster pulse rate.

Clues: mirror; razor blades; rolled-up tin foil or bank notes; drinking straws; white powder; paper wraps; cocaine spoons; needles and syringes (if injected).

Crack

Signs: aggressive, violent behaviour; very excitable and agitated; light hurts eyes.

Clues: small, chalk-like lumps ('rocks'); home-made pipes, from drinks bottles or cans with holes burnt in with a lighted cigarette.

Ecstasy

Signs: boundless energy; depression; feeling very thirsty; being unable to sleep.

Clues: various coloured tablets, about the size and shape of aspirin; drinking huge amounts of soft drinks.

Heroin

Signs: tiny, pinpoint pupils; drowsiness; 'track' marks (see page 46) on body; cramps and sweating (withdrawal); blood stains on clothing or furniture.

Clues: needles and syringes; scorched pieces of tin foil; bent, scorched spoons, or even the disappearance of spoons; used matches; paper wraps; leather thong or rope (for using as a tourniquet); bloodstained cotton wool.

(LSD)

Signs: dilated pupils; unusual perception of sounds and colours; seeing things.

Clues: small squares of paper or tablets; signs of anxiety.

(Solvents)

Signs: more spots or acne than usual; speech is slurred; a terrible, overpowering smell of glue on their breath and on their clothes (even the sniffers themselves can't stand it); brown glue stains on their clothes, especially down the fronts of shirts or trousers; cold sores around their nose and lips (called 'sniffer's rash'); acting in a bizarre way, as if they were drunk.

Clues: empty tubes or cans, maybe hidden under their bed; plastic crisp or carrier bags with traces of glue still on them; the household may be getting through things such as aerosol spray cans of air freshener, furniture polish and hair spray unusually quickly.

WHAT TO DO IF SOMEONE TAKES A DRUGS OVERDOSE

One of the many dangers of drugs is taking an overdose without meaning to (see page 73). If you find a friend, who you know takes drugs, unconscious or very sleepy, they might have taken an overdose. You could save their life if you act quickly and calmly. **Here's what you should do:**

Make sure they get some fresh air – open the windows or doors to let the air in.

Turn them on their side, preferably in the **'recovery'** position (see below). Stay with them if you can in case they are sick. There is always the danger they may choke on their vomit.

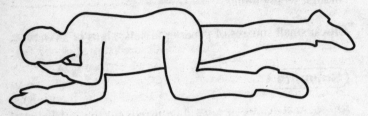

Dial 999 and ask for an ambulance.

Collect any drugs or substances you think they might have been taking – there may be some half-empty bottles or containers lying about – and give them to the ambulance driver. They will be taken to the hospital and will help the doctor know how to treat your friend.

If your friend has been sniffing solvents, try to keep them calm and still. There is a small risk of 'sudden sniffing death' if they get over-excited or start rushing about.

FRIENDS AND PARENTS

"The best thing you can do if your friend, brother or sister, or your son or daughter, does have a problem with drugs is to show them that you care about them, that you want them to get better and that you will support them in their efforts to do so. Don't judge them or blame them for their problem. Saying "It's your own fault" doesn't help anybody. Try to encourage them to get some help. You never know, you might end up saving their life. And, as the

> saying goes, if at first you don't succeed,
> try, try and try again.'
> (A drugs worker)

The effect of having a drug user in the family or among your close circle of friends can be devastating. Your first reaction to the problem might be anger, then sympathy perhaps, then frustration and fear. You don't know what to do, or where to turn to for help. Parents blame themselves, feeling that it must be their fault. If only they'd listened more, or been stricter, or not worked such long hours etc. If it's your brother or sister, you might feel that you've lost them. Their behaviour alters so much, they become so secretive and hostile, that they become different people. You might not be able to talk to them any more, or even like them any more. And you might feel left out, as your parents spend most of their time and energy worrying about them and their problems and don't seem to have any time left over for you.

'One of my kids died from drugs. It seems to me if you dabble in drugs, you die young. It's as simple as that. If you do rehab [rehabilitation treatment], it takes three years to get your life back in order – lost years. My son started with hash etc, then got worse and worse. Then he got on to prescription drugs. Drug addicts are real conners – they fool doctors into giving them drugs. The link between casual, "safe" usage and "hard" drugs is the dangerous thing. There's no such thing as "safe" usage of drugs. Parents need to recognise the problem and confront it, bring it out into the open. The whole family needs counselling.'
(Parent of a young drug user)

One of the things you can do, whether you're a friend, a relative or a parent, is to find out as much as possible about the different types of drugs, the effects they have on people who take them and the sorts of short-term and long-term problems they cause. You'll have had a glimpse of all this in this book. But if you want to know more, you should visit your local library or write off to some of the organisations listed at the back. Many of them will gladly send you leaflets and information packs free of charge, or if you include a stamped, self-addressed envelope. They will also put you in touch with local drugs agencies and advice centres who will talk to you about any problems you come across.

'Being horrified is the wrong reaction for a parent. There's such a mystery attached to drugs. Parents need to get more information and to talk more about the problems. It's no good them blowing their tops – it doesn't have the desired response.'
(Parent of a young drug user)

Self-help groups for helpers

If you suspect someone you know of having a drug problem, you might feel as if you are the only person in the world with such a terrible secret. *DON'T PANIC* – you are not alone. You might try and ignore the problem, hoping that it will go away. When it doesn't disappear, what should you do? If your attempts to help the person involved meet with a hostile reaction, as they very well might, you might feel like giving up and letting them get on with it. *DON'T!* But *DO* find someone to talk to. You need help too if you are going to help the person through their problem. And your life may be disrupted by their use of drugs just as much as their lives are. You need to learn how to cope with the situation, and how not to make it worse. There are self-help groups all over the country where you can learn to do just that. These are groups geared towards the friends and families of drug users. They are places where you can meet other people in the same, or similar, situation to yours and with the same hopes, fears and insecurities. You help each other.

You'll find the names and addresses of various self-help and support groups at the back of the book (pages 175-185).

Dos and don'ts

Here are some practical tips if you find yourself in the situation of having to deal with a close friend or relative who has problems with drugs. They are by no means a complete guide to coping, but they might help to start with.

DON'T blame yourself for someone else's actions. Feeling guilty is quite natural but not very helpful.

DON'T lose your temper and tell the person involved that it's all their fault and that they've only themselves to blame. This will only make matters worse.

DON'T nag the person or lecture them about their behaviour. If they feel they are being 'got at', they may just deliberately lie to avoid confrontation, or go against your wishes for the hell of it.

DON'T cover up for the person or treat them with kid gloves. They've got to face up to the problem, but so have you.

DON'T expect miracles or instant results. Recovery from a drug problem can take a long time. Don't try to hurry it. You will need an enormous amount of patience, and have to deal with lies and disappointments.

DON'T threaten the person with punishments you are not prepared to carry out, such as withdrawing privileges (if you are a parent), or not going around with them (if you are a friend). The person needs to know where they stand. If the rules keep changing, they may feel that there's no point sticking to them in the first place.

DON'T let the person walk all over you or feel they can get away with treating you badly.

DON'T forget about yourself. If you let yourself go, or get too down, you won't be much use to the person you're trying to help.

DON'T ignore problems as they arise. Try to confront them and understand them. That way you acknowledge that they exist – the first step in finding ways of solving them. And now for something more positive...

DO show the person that you care. Tell them that you love them and really want them to get better again.

DO join a self-help group. This way you'll feel less alone and will be able to share your worries and fears with other people who are in the same boat.

DO let people accept their own mistakes. Don't try to pretend that they are your mistakes.

DO take a good look at how you feel and how you are reacting to the problem. Try to be honest about how you feel – there's no point pretending you're fine when you're not.

DO take one day at a time.

DO encourage all attempts at help and support.

If you are a parent:

'Don't react as I did ... I was very angry and it didn't help.'
(A parent)

'Ignorance about drugs can kill.'
(A drugs worker)

'Half the calls we receive are from parents.'
(A drugs counsellor)

If a parent is aware that their son or daughter is sharing illegal drugs with a friend in their house, but does nothing to stop it, they may also be committing an offence.

'We've got to educate people, and learn to deal with the people involved, not just with the substances.'
(A teacher)

'Parents bully and cajole – not the right way to go about helping.'
(A drugs counsellor)

'My father would come home drunk, then my parents would have a row, then I'd go out and get hold of some heroin and feel better. When it got out of hand and I couldn't hide it from them any longer, I was really scared they'd go mad. But they didn't. When I realised my family actually did care about me, I didn't need heroin to make me feel better.'
(16-year-old former heroin user)

You may be tempted to shout and scream, but that will only make matters worse. You have got to show your son or daughter that you are on their side and that they can count on you for help and support. Unless you can trust each other, the problem will take a very long time to go away. You may end up losing your son or daughter altogether. You also need to take care of the rest of the family – it's easy to feel neglected if one person seems to be getting all the attention. And you need to be informed. People often over-react or react in a destructive manner because they don't really know very much about drugs or their effects. All they can think of is that drugs are evil and frightening.

My daughter was about 13 when she got in with the wrong company, really: she had a much older boyfriend with a car; it was a very strong relationship. One night she came home with a girl friend, who stayed the night, and they were talking really late, till about 4.00 a.m.

The next day, Elaine was a bit quiet; then after a bit, she said, "Mum, I need to talk. I'm frightened." She'd been experimenting with drugs, it turned out. She'd taken a trip, LSD, a couple of times and it had been good fun; but the third time she had a really bad experience. That can happen if you're feeling down – and she did. She thought people were after her, hiding in the bushes, really there, really frightening.

Well, I panicked – I didn't know who to go to – we were so close, it really knocked me off my feet. In the end I went to the family doctor, and he gave us a phone number of someone who'd help. This chap talked to the two girls, on their own, and after he'd gone they were just giggling, said he'd just given them advice about how to handle drugs safely; it was OK if you were with a group.

That wasn't really much help – not in dealing with how they felt then and there. So in the end we got some other advice, from Adfam, and we really talked it all through. We talked to the boyfriend and his parents, too, but the main thing was, we talked about the pressure to take drugs, how you feel if the boyfriend puts pressure on, and other friends; if you're not in with a group, you're out, you're on your own. It is so difficult to refuse, even when you don't really want to do it.

Elaine had been getting into trouble in school because she wasn't doing her work; in the end one of the advisers came with us and we talked to the deputy head about the problem. That took some courage, but I'm glad we did it, because eventually the school was able to give us and Elaine some support. At first some of the teachers didn't want to admit there was a drugs problem in the school, but mainly they were really helpful and supportive.

I think the important bit is, how we all talked together. We're more open about it now, and Elaine feels she can always come and ask if anything's worrying her. I've seen parents whose lives have been changed, the pain and agony they go through. But how can you turn your back on someone you really love? But once they're really into it, what do parents know about it? I feel I'm such a lucky Mum, that we've got this relationship – when I think of the way things could have been so much worse.

(Jackie)

Here are a few pointers to bear in mind:

● Try not to let the subject of drugs become a taboo area of conversation. Talking openly about drugs and their related problems will not only show that you are aware of them, but may help to lessen the mystery surrounding them and make them less trendy and attractive.

● Don't just emphasise the harmful or destructive side of drugs. Most people take drugs for pleasure.

● Try not to over-react if you find your son or daughter has been using drugs. This will only push them further away.

● Talk to each other and to the rest of the family about the problem and about their attitudes and responses to it. That way, no one feels left out. After all, it will affect everyone, so everyone has a right to say how they feel.

● Show your son or daughter that you care about them and that you will support them in any way that you can. Try to get them to talk to you, not only about their drug-taking but any other problems which might have contributed to their drug-taking, such as family relationships, peer pressure at school, boyfriend or girlfriend problems, worries about exams etc.

● If they do have problems, try to make constructive suggestions about how they might solve them. For example, encourage them to make new friends, or take up new hobbies or sports. Show them the aspects of their personality that you really value and love. Restoring self-esteem is hugely important.

● If they have a serious problem, try to get them to agree that they need treatment. If they don't, (and they may very well not admit to having a problem), talk to your doctor or to a local drugs advisory centre about what you should do next. There are lots of options open.

● Don't become too suspicious. It may not sound like it from this book, but only a very few young people have problems with drugs. Many never try drugs at all or may only try them once or twice. If you find suspicious-looking tablets in your child's bedroom, remember that they could be aspirin. Don't immediately jump to conclusions.

● Remember that you are dealing with an individual, who is capable of making choices. What they need in order to do that is information, support and a situation of openness and trust.

● Whatever you do, *STAY CALM*. Going berserk will not do you, or them, any good at all.

'Liam: The thing is, you have to know how to handle drugs. If you're smoking, you don't drink – if you mix the two, it's bad news. I hate alcohol, I've seen what it can do to you.

Kate: In the end, it's something about being able to make choices. You have to keep it in perspective and make sure it doesn't overrun your life. You need to know enough, to be aware that drugs can be dangerous... You have to be prepared to take responsibility for yourself.'
(Kate, 16, and Liam, 19)

AN A-Z OF THE LANGUAGE OF DRUGS

A whole language has built up around drugs and the people who use them. There is a vast number of slang words and terms, and these are often different in different parts of the country, and of the world. Terms change, and new ones are introduced, while 'old' ones go out of fashion. Some of the terms may have changed by the time you read this book! However, this is just a selection of some of the words and terms used.

A1 Another name for amphetamines

ACAPULCO GOLD A type of cannabis resin

ACID Another name for LSD

ACID HEAD Someone who uses LSD on a regular basis

ADAM Another name for MDMA (Ecstasy)

AFGHAN BLACK A type of cannabis resin

AFRICAN BUSH A variety of herbal cannabis

AMPHETS An abbreviation for 'amphetamines'

ANGEL DUST Another name for PCP

ANGELS Another name for nitrates

BAD TRIP A bad experience resulting from taking LSD or other hallucinogens

BAG A container used for drugs

BAGMAN Someone who supplies drugs

BANG To inject drugs

BARBS An abbreviation for 'barbiturates'

BASE Another name for crack

BEAT To trick someone out of drugs or money

BENDER A binge of alcohol or drug-taking

BENT Being addicted to drugs

BHANG Another name for cannabis

BIG BROWN ONES Another name for MDMA (Ecstasy)

BIG C Another name for cocaine

BILLY WHIZZ Another name for amphetamines

BLACK A dark type of cannabis resin

BLANKS Poor-quality drugs

BLASTED When you are under the influence of drugs

BLOCK Pieces of cannabis resin

BLOTTERS Another name for LSD

BLOW Another name for cannabis; to smoke cannabis

BLUES Another name for barbiturates

BOMBED When you are high on drugs

BONG A smoking pipe made out of glass for smoking cannabis without using tobacco

BOXED Put in prison

BUFF Another name for money

BURN To trick someone out of drugs or money

BURNED When you have been sold bad-quality drugs

BUSH Another name for cannabis

BUST A raid or arrest by the police

BUZZ The feeling you get when you take drugs

C Another name for cocaine

CANDY Another name for cocaine or for barbiturates

CANNED To be arrested for a drugs offence

CARRIER Someone who buys and sells drugs

CHARLIE Another name for cocaine

CHASING THE DRAGON Smoking heroin

CHINA WHITE Another name for heroin

COASTING When you are under the influence of drugs

COKE Another name for cocaine

COKED UP When you are under the influence of cocaine

COLD TURKEY Withdrawal symptoms from drugs

COMEDOWN When the effect of the drugs wears off

CONNECTION A drug supplier or source of supply

COOK UP To prepare to inject drugs

CRACK A type of cocaine which can be smoked

CRANKING UP A term used for injecting drugs

CUT When a drug is mixed with another drug or substance

DEALER Someone who supplies drugs

DENNIS THE MENACE A type of MDMA (Ecstasy)

DETOX Withdrawing from drugs in a hospital

DIBBLE Another name for the police

DISCO BURGERS Another name for MDMA (Ecstasy)

164

DOPE Another name for cannabis

DOVES A type of MDMA (Ecstasy)

DOWNERS Depressant drugs

DRAGON Another name for heroin (in fact, the fumes given off when heroin is burnt)

DRAW Another name for cannabis

DROP To take LSD by mouth

DUST Another name for PCP or for cocaine

E Another name for MDMA (Ecstasy)

ECSTASY Another name for MDMA

EIGHTH An eighth of an ounce (of cannabis or another drug)

EYE OPENERS Another name for amphetamines

FAST Another name for amphetamines

FINK A person who informs the police about drug deals and dealers

FIX An injection or dose of drugs

FLAKE Another name for crack

FLASHBACK A hallucination which happens days or even weeks or (possibly) years after you have taken a drug

FREAK OUT To have a bad experience with drugs

FREEBASE Another name for crack

FREEBASING Smoking crack

GANJA Another name for cannabis

GEAR Another name for drugs, particularly cannabis

GIMMICKS The equipment used for injecting drugs

GOOFBALLS Another name for barbiturates

GRASS Another name for cannabis buds and leaves

GROOVE To have a good experience with drugs

GUM Another name for opium

H Another name for heroin

HABIT A person's need and use of drugs

HALLUCINATION 'Seeing' things which aren't actually there

HAPPY DUST Another name for cocaine

HARRY Another name for heroin

HASH Another name for cannabis resin

HEAD A person who is addicted to drugs

HERB Another name for cannabis buds and leaves

HIGH When you are under the influence of drugs

HIT A dose or injection of drugs, and the effect

HOOKED To be addicted to drugs

HORSE Another name for heroin

HUFFING Misusing solvents such as glue or aerosols

ICE Another name for cocaine

INDIAN HEMP *Cannabis sativa*, the plant from which cannabis is taken

JACK UP To inject drugs

JOINT A large cannabis cigarette

JUNK Another name for heroin

JUNKIE A person who is addicted to drugs

KICK The effect of a drug

KIT A drug user's equipment

LEBANESE GOLD A type of cannabis resin

LEMONADE A name for bad-quality drugs

LIGHTNING Another name for amphetamines

LINE A dose of cocaine, laid out in a line

LIQUID GOLD Another name for nitrites

LOVE DOVES A type of MDMA (Ecstasy)

M25 Another name for MDMA (Ecstasy)

MAGIC MUSHROOMS Mushrooms which make you hallucinate if you eat them

MAINLINE To inject drugs into your veins

MAN A drugs dealer

MARSHMALLOW Another name for barbiturates

MDMA One form of the amphetamine derivative, Ecstasy

MEET A meeting between a drug user and his or her supplier

MELLOW Another name for LSD

MONKEY Another name for morphine

MOROCCAN GOLD A type of cannabis resin

MOW THE GRASS To smoke some cannabis

MULE A person who carries drugs from one country to another for money

MUNCHIES Feeling uncontrollably hungry after you have been smoking cannabis

NAILED To be arrested by the police

NECKING Swallowing drugs to prevent the police finding them

NEPALESE BLACK A variety of cannabis resin

NEW YORKERS Another name for MDMA (Ecstasy)

OD An overdose of drugs

ON ICE In prison

PAPER MUSHROOMS Another name for LSD

PEACE PILL Another name for PCP

PEDLAR A person who sells drugs

PEP PILLS Another name for amphetamines

PERCY A small quantity of drugs

PINK SKUDS A type of MDMA (Ecstasy)

PLANT A place where drugs are hidden

POPPERS Another name for nitrites

POT Another name for cannabis

PUSHER A person who sells drugs

QUICKSILVER Another name for nitrites

REEFER A cannabis cigarette

ROACH The cardboard filter used in a cannabis cigarette

ROCKS Another name for crack

RUSH The feeling of pleasure which some drugs cause

SCAG Another name for heroin

SCAT Another name for heroin

SCENE The drugs world

SCORE To buy some drugs successfully

SHIT Another name for cannabis

SHOOTING UP Injecting drugs

SKIN Cigarette rolling papers used to make joints

SKIN UP To roll a cannabis cigarette

SKUNK WEED A genetically altered form of cannabis, which is between five and ten times the potency of standard cannabis; causes temporary paralysis

SLEEPERS Another name for barbiturates

SLEIGH-RIDE Another name for cocaine

SMACK Another name for heroin

SNORT Sniff a drug up through the nose

SNOW Another name for cocaine

SNOWBALL A mixture of cocaine and heroin

SPACE CAKE A cake which contains cannabis

SPEED Another name for amphetamines

SPEEDBALL A mixture of cocaine and heroin

SPIKE A needle

SPLIFF A cannabis cigarette

SQUARE Someone who is not involved with drugs

STARDUST Another name for cocaine

STASH A dealer's supply of drugs

STONED When you are under the influence of drugs

STUFF Another name for cannabis or heroin

SUGAR Another name for LSD, because it used to be taken in drops on sugar lumps

SULPHATE Another name for amphetamines

TAB A dose of LSD

TEMPLE BALLS Cannabis oil collected from the mature plant: extremely potent

TORCH UP To light a cannabis cigarette

TRACK To inject into a vein

TRACK MARK The mark left on the skin when drugs are injected into a vein

TRANX Another name for tranquillisers

TRIP Another name for LSD; the experience users have when taking LSD or magic mushrooms

TRUCK DRIVERS Another name for amphetamines

UPPERS Stimulant drugs

WACKY BACCY Another name for cannabis

WALLPAPER Another name for money

WASH Another name for crack

WASTED Under the influence of drugs

WEED Another name for herbal cannabis

WHITE LADY Another name for cocaine

WHIZZ Another name for amphetamines

WIRED TO THE MOON Someone who is high on drugs

WORKS A drug user's equipment

WRAP A small amount of drug sold folded in paper, usually cocaine or amphetamines

WRECKED High on drugs

XTC Another name for MDMA (Ecstacy)

YELLOWS Another name for barbiturates

ZOOM A mixture of amphetamine, heroin and cocaine

PLACES TO GO FOR HELP

There are many places you can go to for help if you need advice or support about a drugs-related problem. Never be afraid to contact someone, however trivial you think your problem may be. They will be only too willing to help you out. Many of them will send you leaflets and information packs free of charge, or they may ask you to provide a stamped addressed envelope.

HELP LOCALLY

Ask your parents for help if you feel you can. Otherwise, you might feel more comfortable asking a doctor or teacher with whom you have a good relationship. If not, there are plenty of other ways of getting help and advice, all of which are confidential.

Look in your telephone book for the telephone numbers of the drug advisory and counselling services in your area. You can also look these up in your local library.

If you are really desperate, you can always phone the Samaritans for help. You'll find the number of your local branch in your telephone book. Alternatively you could call Childline on **0800 1111** or write to them at

Freepost 1111, London, N1 0BR.

Replies will be sent in a plain, handwritten envelope.

HELPLINES

Drink helpline: 0171 332 0202

National AIDS helpline: 0800 567 123
for confidential counselling and advisory services

National Drugs helpline: 0800 77 66 00
a confidential helpline offering advice about drug
and solvent abuse.

National Quitline: 0171 487 3000
for smokers who want to kick the habit

Release: 0171 729 9904
10am – 6pm Monday to Friday
0171 603 8654 (at all other times)

A national drugs and legal service which provides a
24-hour helpline for drug users, their families and friends,
giving confidential advice and information.

Drugs in Schools Helpline: 0345 36 66 66
10am – 5pm Monday to Friday

A confidential nationwide service providing information,
support, advice and assistance to pupils, parents and
teachers in dealing with drug-related incidents in schools.

NATIONAL ORGANISATIONS

ISDD (The Institute for the Study of Drug Dependence)
Waterbridge House
32-36 Loman Street
London
SE1 0EE

0171 928 1211

Library and information service about drug misuse. You can write to them for a list of their publications. They produce lots of quite cheap and very useful booklets, such as **How To Help**.

SCODA (The Standing Committee Conference on Drug Abuse)
Waterbridge House
32-36 Loman Street
London
SE1 0EE

0171 928 9500

National co-ordinating organisation for services for people with drug problems. They produce a booklet called ***Drug Problems: Where to get help*** listing all the services available for drug users and their families. You will find a copy in your local library or Citizens' Advice Bureau.

Health Education Authority
Hamilton House
Mabledon Place
London
WC1H 9TX

0171 383 3833
Customer services **01235 46 55 66**

Provide leaflets on health education, if you phone the customer services telephone number.

Drug Aid
1 Neville Street
Cardiff
CF1 8LP

01222 383 313 (Cardiff)
01685 721 991 (Merthyr Tydfil)
01222 88 1000 (Caerphilly)

For advice and contact numbers if you live in Wales.

Scottish Drugs Forum
5 Oswald Street
Glasgow
G1 5QR

0141 221 1175 (Glasgow)
01382 20 10 16 (Dundee)
0131 220 2584 (Edinburgh)

For advice and contact numbers if you live in Scotland.

Northern Ireland Council for Voluntary Action
127 Ormeau Road
Belfast
BT7 1SH

01232 321 224

Give out contact numbers for advice on substance misuse if you live in Northern Ireland.

Release
388 Old Street
London
EC1V 9LT

0171 729 5255

Give advice about legal problems connected with drug misuse. They also produce lots of very clearly written leaflets about the various drugs and their problems.

Lifeline
101-103 Oldham Street
Manchester
M4 1LW

0161 839 2054

Provide an advice and basic counselling service. Also produce leaflets and information about drugs.

Turning Point
New Loom House
101 Back Church Lane
London
E1 1LU

0171 702 2300

Provide details of local counselling services.

Doddington & Rollo Community Association
Charlotte Despard Avenue
Battersea
London
SW11 5JE

0171 498 4680

A support group for the families and friends of people with drug problems.

Narcotics Anonymous
UK Services Office
PO Box 1980
London
N19 3LS

0171 730 0009 (helpline)
0171 281 99 33 (recorded list of self-help group meetings)

ADFAM (Aid For Addicts and FAMilies)
5th Floor
Epworth House
25 City Road
London
EC1Y 1AA

0171 638 3700

For families and friends of drug abusers.

SOLVENTS

RE-SOLV (The Society for the Prevention of Solvent and Volatile Substance Abuse)
30a High Street
Stone
Staffordshire
ST15 8AW

01785 817 885

A charity concerned with solvent abuse only. They produce leaflets and other information to put you in touch with local advice centres.

National Children's Bureau
Solvent Misuse Project
8 Wakley Street
London
EC1V 7QE

0171 843 6000

Advice on where young solvent abusers can get help.

DRUGS IN SPORT

The Sports Council
Information Centre
16 Upper Woburn Place
London
WC1H 0QP

0171 388 1277

Provides information on drugs in sport and on drug testing.

ALCOHOL

Alcohol Concern
Waterbridge House
32-36 Loman Street
London
SE1 0EE

0171 928 7377

For leaflets and information about alcohol abuse.

AA (Alcoholics Anonymous)
General Service Office
PO Box 1
Stonebow House
Stonebow
York
YO1 2NJ

01904 644 026

Provides contact numbers for local self-help groups and details of meetings.

Alcoholics Anonymous Family Groups UK
61 Dover Street
London
SE1 4YS

0171 403 0888

Advice and support for the family and friends of people with drink problems.

DRUGS AND AIDS

Mainliners
205 Stockwell Road
London
SW9 9SL

0171 737 3141

Advice line for people with HIV resulting from drug misuse.

Terrence Higgins Trust
52-54 Gray's Inn Road
London
WC1X 8JU

0171 831 0330

Support group for people with HIV and AIDS. You can also
contact them for information.

SMOKING

ASH (Action on Smoking and Health)
109 Gloucester Place
London
W1H 4EJ

0171 935 3519

Organisation campaigning against smoking.

COUNSELLING SERVICES

BAC (British Association for Counselling)
1 Regents Place
Rugby
CV21 2BS

Will send information on local counselling services if you provide an A4 SAE.

Notes

Notes

_____

_____

_____

_____

_____

_____

_____

_____

_____

_____

_____

_____

_____

_____

_____

Reference Point is a mega new series, with all the info you need on issues that affect *you*.

Available now:
Star Signs. What are you like? Find out about you, your friends and family – and whether you believe in stars at all.

Look out for:
Memory. *It* never, ever forgets, but *you* do. Find out how to make the most of your memory, and uncover some incredible mysteries of the mind.

Fat. Take the weight off your mind and wise up to some amazing truths about diets, food and how you really look. With true experiences.

Discover the points of YOU.

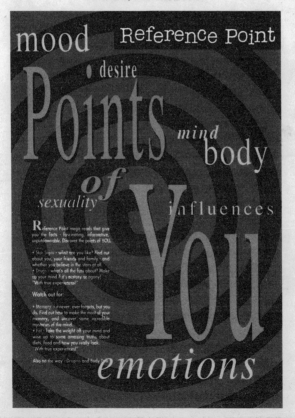